LIFE ETERNAL

LIFE ETERNAL

Communicated by
W. T. STEAD

And recorded by
ESTELLE STEAD

WHITE CROW

www.whitecrowbooks.com

William Thomas Stead

Contents

～

Introductory Note

~

The writings included in this book have been "inspired" by my father during the last four years. Prior to that, for some time, he had constantly been telling us, that he was anxious to write a book, which would logically follow *The Blue Island* – not a sequel to it, but an enlargement, an explanation of it. To some, as he says, his explanation may be a disappointment, but it certainly seems feasible and natural, that there must be a time of readjustment after the change brought about by the death of the physical body. This time of adjustment is spoken of as the "Plane of Illusion", by F. W. H. Myers, in *The Road to Immortality*.

People will ask: "How do I know these writings come from my father?" He has proved this satisfactorily to me in many ways, 1, by confirmation and directions given through other mediums, two, by proof given to myself alone – for at times I can see him and hear him speak. Most convincing of all was the fact that as I sat by Mrs. Dowden, watching the writing, a strong feeling of his presence pervaded the room. There was no mistaking it – he was there. I was as conscious of his presence and his personality, as I was in the old days, when he would walk up and down in his sanctum dictating and talking to me when I acted as his secretary. In the production of the writing there was no hesitation, he had what he wished to say ready, and it came through quickly and concisely, even when months elapsed between the sittings, he commenced from where he had left off, and carried on as if there had been no interval.

When here, it was always his wish to reach "The Man in the Street", and I know that it was "The Man in the Street" that he had in his mind when writing this book. It has been his aim to give him a wider outlook, and to explain some of the mysteries that surround us during our life here, and in the Great Beyond, to give him a grasp of the vastness, the intelligence behind, the order of, and the wonder of Life – Life Eternal, in a way that should appeal to him.

As he says, he is writing as a traveller, who is journeying through the mysteries that lie outside the world, only a little further on in Life's voyage, and that on no subject can his words be taken as final.

Then we must realize that there is so much that cannot be given, because of our limitations in words and expression. Also we must remember that from where he is writing, there are still differences of opinion.

He has told us, that they have great discussions with reference to the matter that can be, and shall be written, and that what he writes is not his opinion alone, but voices the opinions and experiences of many on the other side.

The second part, "Communication between the Spheres," was given first. He seemed to find more difficulty in explaining this, possibly because it is of a more technical nature and, although he was keenly interested and anxious to transmit it for the help he hopes it will afford to students and researchers, I know that he feels it will not have the same appeal to the general reader as Part 1.

He seemed to have much greater joy in giving these later writings, which, by his request, are now put first.

After the book was finished, he insisted on our gathering together a group of people, some of whom had given much time and thought to psychic research, while others had but little knowledge. He was anxious, he said, to see how the different minds reacted to it, he wished to read their thoughts, answer their questions, and in this way judge of its general appeal. When here he was always keen on discussions and questions, he considered these the best means of getting to the root of what is really wanted.

In this respect he has not changed. When giving the scripts he would inquire as to the kind of questions usually put by students, so that he might help by answering them. He urged the members of the group to ask questions. As you read no doubt many questions will crowd into your minds, and we hope that you will find some of these answered in the lists of "Questions and Answers" given at the end of most of the chapters. It is his hope that the subject matter of this book will be widely discussed and, compared with other views that have come through from his side.

This book comes to you with his greetings, and those of his collaborators. It is their earnest wish that it may help towards a better understanding and a clearer insight into that most wonderful of all mysteries – Life, Life Eternal.

Before closing I must express our gratitude, my father's and mine, to the one who so kindly lent her hand that the writings might be given, and to Mr. Stanley de Brath for his foreword.

ESTELLE W. STEAD.

5, Smith Square,
Westminster,
London, S.W.1.
May 16th, 1933.

Note by the Automatist

~

In writing the book which follows, my sensations have been those of a secretary who is taking down intricate and difficult ideas, translated into clear and simple language, reading as she writes. I have never been so fully conscious of the presence of a communicator as in the W. T. Stead case. I feel that he is entirely outside my own personality, using me as an instrument with infinite skill. I find myself conversing with him exactly as I should if his bodily presence was beside me, discussing difficult problems and often even arguing with him.

It has been a very pleasant task to record what I hope will be a valuable addition to our understanding of psychic phenomena. I must thank my communicator for using me so swiftly – the pace at which he writes is about 3,000 words an hour, which entirely prohibits any thinking process on my part.

Great care has been taken by W. T. Stead to make his ideas clear to his readers. Again and again we have been asked whether we can follow what he has written, and he himself suggested that the book should be read aloud to an intelligent circle of investigators and fully discussed, when doubtful points were cleared up by the communicator in automatic writing.

I hope that his readers will find the book as interesting as his automatist has found it.

HESTER DOWDEN.

15, Cheyne Gardens,
Chelsea.

Foreword

~

When Miss Stead asked me to write a foreword to this book, I was very doubtful of my ability to meet her wishes.

Any adequate foreword should ordinarily imply a certain superiority to, or at least familiarity with, the matter commented on. That can hardly be the position of anyone in Earth life, with respect to the communications from the standpoint of one who, after an Earth life of full and unselfish endeavour, has passed to the Life Beyond. To such we must always be learners. This is doubly the case when the communicator envisages such a vast subject as the progress of the soul in the "spheres" of the fuller life, and attempts the task of showing this to beings who are as yet in the infantile Earth stage.

But when I came to read the epilogue which deals with the effect of the new knowledge, I found myself in such complete agreement with it, that I took heart to write the foreword which Miss Stead was kind enough to ask me for. Professor John MacMurray told us in the *Listener* of January 13th, 1933, that we "neither believe nor disbelieve . . . and this paralyses our capacity to decide and to act ".

If this is emphatically true in the world of finance (where there is ample excuse for uncertainty) and in the world of religious dogmatism, where we must rest on authority; it is certainly not true as regards our life and death. We shall die! But curiously enough, that certainty is not counterbalanced by the fact that we shall certainly live! Sir Oliver Lodge and Professor Hyslop have both declared that Survival is *scientifically* proven. Sir Oliver Lodge could hardly be more emphatic than he has been in the epilogue to *The Bridge*, where he says: "That occasional communion is possible between those still associated with matter, and those who have entered on another phase of existence, – these things are to me not hypothetical or doubtful, but definite and scientifically ascertained facts. ... I do not propose to qualify the statement with any apology or hesitation, for I am as convinced of these things as of any other facts of nature, and I feel sure that posterity will realize their truth." What we do need is to realize Survival as a fact, and not as a theory which may or may not be true.

We need to counterbalance this by another fact, that as we live here so do we develop our mental powers (or fail to develop them) so that we apprehend (or fail to apprehend) the new environment into which we enter, and accordingly find in it happiness or misery.

This is not difficult to realize. One of the faculties of the new life is the power to read the thoughts of those whom we may meet. All thought is naked and open. We can easily perceive that this may be the cause of the highest delight or of the greatest humiliation. It depends on ourselves.

Knowing the great difficulty of presenting the very complex facts of the new life through any medium (even through so proven a medium as Mrs. Hester Dowden), and the imperfections of human language on what we may call the physics of soul-life, it was not to be expected that the opening chapters should be other than somewhat obscure. That *The Blue Island* should be described as a land of illusion was not surprising, – I always felt it to be so. And that the next phase of human development should be described as a birth into a world of illusion – which has been developed in some recent communications purporting to be from F. W. H. Myers – is scarcely more than the statement that Earth life is also illusion, which is the general experience of Oriental philosophy. Every advance in comprehension must regard past stages as illusory. This does not make them any less real to those who are in each stage.

Reality might be defined as the correspondence between the senses and the objects perceived by them and interpreted by the mind. All childhood is illusory, its joys, its pains, its experiences are real to the child, but illusory to the adult. So Earth life is felt to be Maya – illusion – by those who have advanced to a higher state. In Earth life we are learning, and must not take anything expressible in earthly language as final truth.

To the earthly mind there is fortunately no finality.

Part 1 (Life After Death) is much more readily comprehensible than Part 2. I should advise all serious students to read the former Part and the epilogue, carefully, before tackling the more intricate Part 2. The woven garments described in Chapter 1, para. 2, are curiously borne out in some photographs by Dr. Glen Hamilton reproduced in *Psychic Science* of January 1st, 1933. Examination of the figures in that issue with a strong hand magnifier, will show that the Ectoplasm in which the face and hair appears, is a woven textile. (This is much clearer in the original stereograph than in the print from a process-block.) Where, and by whom, was it woven? The description in Chapter 1, Part 1, is borne out by many other communications, and the whole book should be a valuable aid to those who desire to know as much as can be told of the new life which we are all destined to inherit.

Another point which is not directly mentioned in the book, is the nature of time and reality. I take the latter first: Reality is the environment which corresponds to our faculties on any grade of being. It may be impermanent, but it is always objective, though related to the subjective in that grade. This material world is objective and very real to us, though impermanent.

All the talk (mathematical and otherwise) about the nature of matter and time, is a reaching out after the absolute. It does not alter by one iota the facts or sequences which we call the "laws of nature" by which our machines work, trains run, and on which all our civilization and daily life are founded. If we miss the last tube-train home, no consideration of space-time will help us! All our civilization is founded in normal atomic chemistry. The discovery of the electron does not invalidate Dalton's Atomic Law.

As soon as we touch electrons, protons, radioactivity, and quanta, we enter on another non-material world. These infinitesimally small quantities, many hundreds of diameters below our powers of microscopic vision, have laws of their own which we have not yet discovered, but they are not the laws of atomic matter. Their world is historically antecedent to the formation of the first hydrogen molecule at a temperature of perhaps 100,000° C. in a blue star. The expulsion of an electron from a helium atom is possible, and radium may be convertible into lead on a minute scale in the laboratory, but these phenomena only show a link between the material and the nonmaterial worlds. The world of energy is probably part of that non-material world of Matter. Gravitation, electricity, magnetism, heat, light, chemical affinity, muscular or nervous power, and radioactivity are all invisible apart from Matter, inter-convertible in exact equivalents, and each can fill a whole space without making it impenetrable to other forms of energy. A room may be full of luminous vibrations, music, wireless and cosmic vibrations of all kinds without mutual interference. These belong to the immaterial world, and are links with this. They are not liable to decay, and, apart from matter, are timeless.

Time as relative to this world, is measured by the day and year, the result of planetary movement, but duration is independent of any such movement, and is subjective though not unreal. Time is also measured by the swing of the pendulum, which is correlated to planetary movement, for the second of time is but a small fraction of the 24 hours. The time for one swing is 3.1416 length of pendulum, intensity of gravity, and this is inseparable from our standards of length and mass.

What I am endeavouring to bring out is that there are three discrete but connected worlds lying within the range of our perceptions:

(*1*) The physical world, whose sequences are common experience and well known to normal science.

(2) The world of physical causation – Energy. The laws of this world, though not their causes, are also fairly well known to

normal science, so long as the forms of Energy are associated with matter. Energy is "granular", composed of quanta, but of its behaviour in "free space" as radiation, we know but little.

(3) The world of life, which uses both the above as its perceptible basis, also for its maintenance. To it belong Beauty, Goodness, and Truth, all these being inter-related and each productive of the others. The want of them, or their opposites, are the prime cause of the fall of nations. That world is limitless.

Each of these interpenetrates with the other two, and at death the average "good" man passes with extended faculties, into a region in which space and time is but a mathematical symbol for an order of things which we cannot translate into psychical symbolism. In that region perception is superior to both space and time: we "see" through material things, our vision is not limited to surfaces as in this world: we have not quite lost touch with matter, but it is a more refined form (ectoplasm?) and is ideo-plastic – capable of being influenced directly by Mind. Of this form of matter we know very little.

Everything in this present world is relative to our faculties, not absolute – not untrue, nor unreal, but impermanent, except the last. These facts underlie all Spiritualist problems. They do not make the Bible story untrue, but relative to the men for whom it was designed. Monism is logically and philosophically true. From God – the Universal Creative Power – all worlds and all life proceed. Not by any such process as the allegory of Genesis, or even directly, as if there were no intelligences between God and man. Christ is the revelation of that Power to the world. He came from a higher sphere where Beauty, Goodness, and Truth are allied to a Wisdom which to our phase of evolution seems perfect. Therefore His main teaching – Truthfulness, Clean living, and Kindliness are the first essentials to our progress towards those higher spheres.

Truthfulness means much more than abstention from lies, spoken or acted. Clean living means much more than honest sexual relations: it covers abstention from the gambling which is the poison in commercial and social life. Kindliness is the conduct which results from the knowledge that Humanity is one unit. It means the solidarity of mankind.

In this time of severe stress, these are our only way out. This book should aid in opening the minds of all men to these facts, and should show the real unity of Religion and Science.

STANLEY DE BRATH.

Kew,
January, 1933.

PART 1

LIFE ETERNAL

~

Introduction

~

In writing the following pages I find myself in a difficulty, which is in a sense insuperable. I am going to attempt that which might at first appear impossible, i.e., endeavour to describe an entirely different condition, from that in which my readers now live. I am going to use the language of the inhabitants of the Earth, although here in my sphere language is no longer a necessity. Therefore, allowance must be made, if what I describe at times seems grossly material.

Limitations

I cannot paint my picture, or read my verse, if I do not use materials which appeal to your understanding.

In my case materials are words. If I speak of food or drink, houses, poverty, wealth, you must not take it that what I speak of is precisely the equivalent of your poverty and wealth, your food and drink, your houses, etc., I can but do my best, and when I have finished this book, you will understand that my knowledge is limited, that there is an infinity to learn, that the limitations under which I am working, are very similar to those from which you suffer.

Facts about "The Blue Island"

I shall, in the beginning, try to explain the meaning of *The Blue Island*, which is the prelude to this book. I have, in writing *The Blue Island*, given no indication that it is not a fact, that it represents an actual sphere, a world of the reality of our own. It does exist, as all that which is called delusion, is also reality, the dividing line is not clearly marked for the living. There are two realities. The reality that is outside the soul, and the greater reality that is within it. The reality without, I shall hereafter call the delusion or the image. For the reality within I will retain the term "reality", which describes it best in your language. I shall speak of planes and spheres, and here I may as well explain these terms as I understand them. But my readers will always bear in mind that I am writing as a traveller through the mysteries that lie outside the world, and that on no subject can my words be taken as final.

The Spheres

Sphere suggests a circle, the globe, the spheroid that is the shape of the world you live in. Put that image from your mind, for it indeed is a delusion.

The spheres are not shapes, they are not countries, they are not worlds, they are different states or conditions through which the soul passes on its way back to the great central force which is God. We speak of seven spheres, seven different states, and in each of these there are seven planes. The spheres are of different quality, and the duration of the soul's sojourn in each is of a different length. The state which I call a sphere, is a mental condition. In each of the spheres we retain "form". Our bodies become more ethereal as we ascend, or, if our choice prompts us to descend, we have more material bodies. These "forms" are given us so that we may preserve a shape until, the spirit being set free after we pass the seventh sphere, we are merely part of the great central plan and no longer preserve our personality.

The Planes

The planes are, in fact, immense groups of individual souls inhabiting the spheres. In your world you speak of nationalities: we have our nationalities also, but with this difference – ours are the nationalities of the soul. We are divided into countries according to our mental condition. But we are not white and black, English and Chinese, as you are.

In a former book, I spoke of teachers, leaders and guides who are always with us during our life on Earth, as well as our other lives, but they are objective to the soul. Therefore, as they do not exist in the inner soul, I speak of them as an image that is invisible after we begin the life after death. I do not mean by this that we never see them, we do under certain circumstances, when we first arrive, and when we are at séances.

The Reality Within

I make these very imperfect explanations so that my preface may act as a glossary for my readers, they will understand in which sense these terms are used, and they will no longer fail to realize that the greater reality is within the soul. The soul creates reality within itself, as it evolves. By reality, I mean conviction, a certainty arrived at by the inner mind, of another life and another sphere beyond the one in which it dwells at the moment, and that certainty is arrived at through glimpses of that sphere beyond.

You call your realities imagination and delusion.

You are quite unaware that you are looking as it were through an open door, at the sphere above you.

Touch, smell, and taste, to you seem realities. Consider that touch, smell, and taste are passing sensations. The sphere which you can see through the eyes of your mind, is unchanging and eternal. I want to put you all on a firm basis as far as I can. I don't want to use terms, the value of which, you are unable to understand. So far as my experience goes, I want you to travel with me and see things through my eyes.

The Blue Island: A Dream State

In *The Blue Island* I tried to describe a state that "carried us over" a period following a shattering shock, and a great and sudden change. As a matter of fact a "cure" was being accomplished, and this being wrought, we arose, awoke, rubbed our eyes, and found ourselves in a world not so unlike your own: a world in which we all felt awkward and strange at first. Then we knew that The Blue Island was a dream common to all of us, and that now we should go on our separate ways, and begin our new life. 1 I suppose you will think that we knew we were dead, that we remembered our last moments on the ship, and that our memories remained perfect. Well you assume too much. My first sensation on waking up, was pretty much that of a baby who rubs his eyes, and begins to cry. I felt almost uncomfortable, puzzled, dazed, and yet I was conscious of uncommon youth and vigour. I felt that I must get up and move about.

Surely movement would be a different thing now, with such an access of strength. Remember? Yes, I remembered my life and the ship as I remembered my childhood when I was alive. I wasn't a bit surprised when my father walked into the room and took me by the hand.

Sudden Death, its Effect on the Soul

After death the soul shoots out of the body, inflicting a terrific strain on itself. The cord uniting the soul with the body, which resembles the cord between the mother and child, is not always severed at the moment of death, as a rule it is, but there are exceptions, and the term of severance depends to a certain extent on the knowledge the soul possesses of its conditions. With sudden death, the shock being great, the term of severance may be delayed for a long period, but this is the exception not the rule, in most cases of sudden death the cord is severed at once.

---

[1] See *The Blue Island*, Chapter xii.

A period of confusion follows sudden death in either case. When the cord is not severed at once the soul is bound to the body, and this prevents it deriving benefit from the curative conditions to which it is taken. Will you try to realize with me, that The Blue Island was not uniform to us all? Some were quite unable to get up and enjoy the delights of the sea and bathing. They were too inert to move or go about. Comparable to cases you come across on your side of people who succumb to inertia, or lack of "will to live" as in extreme anaemia.

Those who were wise helped the snapping of the cord, by their desire to use and enjoy their temporary conditions. This they did instinctively and felt the benefit at once.

Have I disappointed you all by saying that in my sense of the term, The Blue Island was a delusion? Dreams are an essential for all of us during life on Earth, and are still more essential when we cast off the body. But for our dreams we could not continue our journey, for in the world of dream the soul finds rest from the sharper realities within itself.

Questions and Answers

Q. You say you woke up and rubbed your eyes, but in The Blue Island you say you woke and knew all about it. Explain.

A. I have always tried to say exactly what I felt. After death, that is immediately after, while the soul still clings partly to the body, it realizes what has happened. At times I realized it. I was then speaking of the hours that followed the shipwreck. I now speak of the beginning of my new life as a complete personality.

Q. You say that in dreams we touch reality, do you mean in all dreams?

A. That does not apply to all dreams. I am speaking here of that which is almost the equivalent of trance in the Earth sphere. Holding back the full consciousness will do.

Q. Am I right in supposing spheres and planes depend on rates of vibration?

A. Quite true. I gave the impression I fear that spheres and planes are one and the same thing, whereas planes are steps through one extension of consciousness. There comes a break and a wider extension is reached. I should call the condition after the break the higher sphere.

Q. On one occasion Professor Tyndall while lecturing at the Royal Institution received a violent shock from the large battery of Leyden jars belonging to the laboratory. He did not lose consciousness, but for some time felt as if his arms and legs were detached from his body and functioning in space, though still under his control. After a time they seemed to be drawn in again and become normal. Would it be a similar sensation to the sense of confusion after sudden death?

A. Yes, precisely. We feel when this occurs that we have no actual shape, limbs we may have, but no heart or lungs.

1

The Source of Life

~

In starting this book, I would first speak of the great Ancestor from whom all life is generated. What I say will be purely theoretical because God is unknown to us at my stage, or at any stage, in the seven spheres.

I can, however, be definite as to Him being the source of life, and I shall try to trace the spiritual family down from Him, through the seven groups of which we have definite knowledge.

A knowledge of your spiritual parentage and relationship will help you to understand the meaning of your likes and dislikes, your loves and hates. It is a difficult subject to compress into one short chapter, but I will do my best to give you some idea of the wonder of it.

Our Great Spiritual Ancestor

We are all descended from one great Spiritual Parent who is both Father and Mother to the whole universe, but I should not speak of this great source of life as a parent – the word "ancestor" gives you my meaning better. The whole universe had one great Spiritual Ancestor, and that Ancestor has begotten seven, who form the seven great primitive groups which may be symbolized as the Archangels. From these seven primitive ancestors an infinite number of new groups are formed and a long line of descent can be traced from the original Ancestor through the seven who are part of Him, and from them through an ever-increasing stream of life.

You ask, are all seven your spiritual ancestors and mine? Yes, but indirectly. The life stream flows down to us from them but we must descend a long way through that stream of life before we find our actual parents, the father and mother of our spirit from whom we, as individuals, are born.

The group to which we belong, to which we owe our individuality, has its source in a bi-sexual portion of the stream, splitting away from it, and again subdividing into many parts.

Now let us take the situation with regard to the spheres. Life had divided itself into seven parts before it descended into any of the spheres. It continues to be a united affinity both male and female, until it enters the fifth sphere. The moment it enters this new atmosphere it splits again, and this time into male and female.

Our Spiritual Parents

The original split in the fifth sphere gives you your spiritual parents. Your spiritual parents are the two parts of that which was one, until it broke asunder in the fifth sphere to come down as two separate streams through the remaining four spheres, into the physical.

These two streams are continually forming new splits, increasing the spiritual family as new spheres are touched, and always breaking into male and female.

When the streams of the family have descended and arrived at the physical – have come down to Earth as it were – the spiritual groups which are male and female await actual birth into the Earth sphere, and they incarnate as quickly as they can.

Our Physical Parents

We are told that in the beginning, the physical parents were formed when the spiritual family was ready, but no one has any actual knowledge of where the physical parents came from. I believe, that when evolution at last produced man, the spiritual family first entered into the physical. And that the real difference between animals and human beings is, that animals have no spiritual ancestry. Personality begins when the spirit enters the physical. Let me describe it in this way. Imagine a stream flowing rapidly down a mountain. When the water reaches the plain it splits into many sprays. Take this as the spiritual stream that has its group individuality but does not take on individuality in its atoms until it reaches the physical.

The Law of Spirit

The law of the spirit, is that it must descend from the greater life 'through many channels, until it reaches the Earth sphere, which is the lowest it can touch, and from the Earth sphere, it must retrace its steps, first through physical incarnation, and later through mental and spiritual incarnations, until it again attains the height from which it descended originally.

Your real ancestors, your real forebears, are those who were related to you before you entered into incarnation in the Earth sphere. The physical incarnation will give you physical relatives, but it is quite possible that not one of these will be related to you spiritually. Those who are instinctively attracted to you, and those who instinctively attract you, are your real family. You should obey these inclinations and should not be in bondage to the physical family. The physical family may, and indeed must, claim your care and consideration, and so far as you can, you must provide for them, but they are not yours unless by some fortunate chance they are related to you spiritually. Your real family come to you of their own free will, and are not in bondage in any sense, it is an entirely instinctive drawing together. The physical family is the pattern of the spiritual. You will have relatives in the spiritual family who are close or distant, and you may find one who is the other part of yourself who may be called your affinity.

Now I feel I have said all that can be digested in a book which deals with generalities.

Questions and Answers

Q. How about planetary influences?

A. The seven original ancestors represent the planets and rule our destinies to a certain extent because we carry within us the characteristics of whichever of these gave us our spiritual ancestry.

Q. What about planetary constellation at birth?

A. Those that mark your destiny are all related to each other. You have one special planetary influence which governs you in the main, but as, in a family, relationships influence each other, so the planets influence each other.

2

The Soul

~

The Soul: What is it? Few people who have used this word
can define it. Firstly, I want to explain that we are threefold
while we are on Earth. We are body, soul, and spirit. The
body I need not define, but I shall lay great stress on the nature of
the soul apart from the spirit.

The Physical Body's Relation to the Soul

Let us take the man living on Earth. He is conscious of his body, he
is also conscious of his mind working through the physical brain:
but though he uses the word "soul" very glibly to express that part
of himself which may possibly survive death, he cannot define the
term. He visualizes the soul as an infant body within his own, for
he is quite sure that the soul is smaller than he is. I should like him,
for his better understanding to realize exactly how his physical body
stands in relation to his soul.

When I talk of the soul I mean the entire individuality, the ego,
the "I" that is at all times, and which is indestructible. When I speak
of the body worn whilst on Earth, I use the word as I should coat or

garment, for it is destructible and will decay after the soul leaves it. Thus the body means nothing more than the house which the soul inhabits while it is on Earth. Our houses on Earth are larger than we are, we live within them, but the soul is a million times larger and greater than his earthly home, and this dwelling place which he inhabits for a short time suffers because of his size and extent.

What I say seems an impossibility. Do not reject it and I will try to make my meaning clear. The soul, being the whole personality, has a knowledge of the purpose for which it was created, it has also a knowledge of the development that is before it, but this knowledge is subconscious. And by subconscious, I mean that it does not take this knowledge into the part of its consciousness that is active. While a man is on Earth, he only needs a fraction of his personality.

All the rest of his personality is there, but as it is not necessary to use it, it remains in a trance condition.

Man only Conscious of One-Seventh of his full Personality

Thus we may say, that while man is on the Earth, he is not conscious of his soul. But the soul is life, and if it leaves the body for a moment, the body must either sleep or die. When the soul leaves the body in sleep, it immediately becomes conscious of two sevenths of its personality, whereas on Earth it is conscious of one-seventh only. When it leaves the Earth body permanently, it enters only into the consciousness it had when the body was asleep. It has no consciousness of the remaining five-sevenths of itself.

You can visualize the seven worlds through which we must travel as seven glass globes, each being twice the size of the one which precedes it. The soul knows the sphere it is in, it also knows those which are below its present abode, but it is still unconscious of those which are above it.

Object of the Journey through the Spheres

Now what is the object of the journey through the spheres? It is a long journey, for as you ascend to higher spheres, life is doubled in length. My life will be twice as long in the sphere I am in at this moment, as it was on the Earth. The object of the long journey is to gain complete realization of the soul, or personality. Until we know ourselves, we cannot be said to have reached maturity.

You will ask: is the progress painful, does the soul suffer in the realization of itself? No, it gains by every extension of its consciousness, gains in happiness, in security, in balance. By happiness, I mean the elimination of fear.

You infants in the nursery of the Earth, suffer from a disease called fear, which is in reality, ignorance. As you ascend you will gradually cast off your fear.

When you pass on to the sphere above the Earth sphere, you will have lost the fear of physical illness and death, for instance.

Free will Limited

When it reaches the seventh sphere, the soul has full realization of itself. It understands its purpose, and then it is free to choose its destiny. It is no longer hampered by the laws which compel it to take the next step. It can choose its own road. But before that, free will is limited. It must advance, unless it is sufficiently foolish to wish to retrace its footsteps. This does sometimes occur, but not often, and almost invariably the causes of its return are childish. This will disappoint those who believe they have had many lives on Earth, but it is none the less true. It is the love of the past which calls the soul back to the spheres it has left. It is willing to lose the extension of the consciousness it has gained, and compress itself once more into the very ill-fitting garment of the body, in order to experience familiar sensations again. I shall not enter into the subject of reincarnation here, as I have written about it in a separate chapter. At this point I am occupied with the soul, and its steady and uninterrupted journey through the spheres.

It gains knowledge of itself and life concurrently, for it becomes more and more alive as it ascends. It learns now, not through the physical brain, but through a brain that is part of its new body, which gives the mind a better chance of functioning.

The Mind the Eye of the Soul

I must now define the word "mind" as apart from soul, and the word "spirit" as apart from either. The soul, as I have said, is the whole individuality. The mind might be described as the eye of the soul, for the soul directs its life force on the brain and functions through it for the needs of the consciousness. The word "mind" as I use it means the soul functioning through the physical brain. The body we wear after we leave the Earth, has a similar apparatus to the brain, and the soul uses this through which to send its purposes.

Spirit, the Life Which Animates the Whole

Let us leave the mind, and turn to the spirit. What is the spirit apart from the soul? The spirit is not apart from the soul – it is the life which animates the whole personality. What that life is, we cannot tell, not even if we have ascended to the seventh sphere.

Call it Life, call it God, it is beyond our comprehension. I give these definitions, because if I use the word "soul", "spirit" or "mind", I want you to understand the sense in which I use them.

As the soul ascends, it uses a more delicate instrument for the mind to function through, so that when the higher spheres are reached, knowing without learning is attained, or in other words, all knowledge becomes intuitive. Of that high stage of development, I have no experience, of course, but I may say here, that those who, through exercises such as are used in the East, try to attain intuition before their time, run a risk which they cannot appreciate.

The Purpose of the Soul

What is the object of the journey? Shall we go to the end and look at the goal before we travel the road? The object is, first as I have said, to arrive at full realization of the soul, but after that, is there no road to be travelled? The journey has been long, the highest pinnacle has been reached. What is the purpose of the soul? Perhaps you will be surprised when I say simply that it has now reached absolute free will. At last it is not subjected to any natural law. It can do as it pleases. It realizes that, if it pleases, it can pass into the Greater Life. This will not mean death. It will probably mean ecstasy, and the soul functions in a state of active happiness.

But those who have reached the pinnacle, and who, in their journey, have learned to pity and love their fellows, are not likely to pass on to this state of bliss.

They will want to go back, and help some of the travellers in the lower spheres. These are the guides and helpers, who work in groups, who try to shorten the journey for their struggling fellows. These are the artists who inspire younger souls who are struggling with music, with colour, with words. Then there are a few – very few in comparison with those who become guides and controls – who feel that the journey has been so full of interest that it is worthwhile to travel the whole road again, with the greater knowledge they have acquired. These are the supermen, the great artists, warriors, and saints. Some people are born into the Earth sphere with much higher development, much better equipment than others. So many grades of intelligence are found on Earth, that the question naturally arises, have these people been here before? Are these cases of reincarnation? Yes, that accounts for some cases, but not for all.

Some souls enter the Earth sphere with a more adult mentality than others, but they may be held up later on, while the less intelligent minds advance and get even with them.

What do the seven spheres represent? The Earth may be likened to the Tower of Babel, so much chaos is there, so many apparent injustices. But please remember it is the lowest stratum in the order of development. In the third, fourth, fifth and sixth spheres, order is gradually evolved, shall we call it a sorting out? Some of the less highly developed souls may, and indeed will, extend as they rise. But the sorting out of which I speak is not a dividing up of the wise and the foolish, but a division of life for the special purpose for which it was created. As you ascend, there is no longer a mixture of human beings who cannot understand each other. The souls who benefit each other are drawn together, as the coloured glass of a kaleidoscope forms itself into symmetrical patterns. The sphere beyond the Earth, is the first step towards group formation. The Tower of Babel is not quite such a hopeless confusion as it was on Earth.

Gradually as you ascend conditions become calmer and clearer. The mind is used less, you remember what that word means. The soul begins to function more and more independently.

The Length of the Journey

So you pass from one sphere to another, and though you have not reached Heaven, you begin to ask yourself what Heaven may mean. You may ask how long this journey takes. If it is continuous and uninterrupted, life will be twice as long in each succeeding sphere as in the sphere that precedes it. That will give you a mathematical problem which I do not propose to solve for you at the moment. Can anything interrupt the journey or retard the progress? Indolence, which may take hold of you at any moment, or a childish harping back to the past, which may drive you to reincarnate. These are the chief causes of delay.

You may be delayed of your own free will, because you feel you have not exhausted some special study in one of the spheres, but that merely means that you are long lived at that stage of development.

Questions and Answers

Q. Doesn't one miss the "rub" in a world of similar tastes?

A. No, that is not so. You meet the people who differ from you at all times, but after the Earth sphere is past there is no longer the preposterous melee of tastes and interests there was in the first incarnation. Remember it is only one step forward.

Q. Why are there such great differences on Earth, and how is that levelled up?

A. That is all compensated for at a later stage of development. The earlier stage is merely the first steps: when you take four steps your debts are being settled.

Q. But why should there be such differences?

A. That depends upon the matter of which the soul is made. It enters its natural place in the world. You may ask why I say "natural". You must see that the material out of which human beings are made, is different.

Q. Why should fine characters be born into a degrading environment?

A. So that they may rise up from that environment, and through their strength help those around them to rise. In this way they rid themselves of much they would have to endure in other lives.

Q. Do you mean future lives in other spheres?

A. Yes, I do not mean other lives on Earth.

Q. Do they choose the bodies they are to inhabit?

A. No, they do not choose: they drift automatically according to the law of the attraction of particles.

Q. Is there any special purpose behind the Earth life?

A. Purpose is hardly the way I should put it, and yet I suppose it expresses what you mean, but I should call it reason. Yes, there is a purpose. Imagine that the sun sends forth millions of fragments, some small, some large, of different shape and kinds. The object of these sparks, at some time in their future, is to re-enter the body of the parent sun, but in itself, each has its image and its potentialities. Now the lesser ones will find it slower and more difficult to return to the parent body than the greater. The force that sent them out, was like the breath of the parent's nostrils. It was not conscious of a special purpose for each, but for all.

Q. Why should the breath come out unevenly?

A. Why, indeed? We cannot explain, but we know there is no waste in the universe, and that all these sparks will be perfected before they re-enter the whole.

Q. Why do some people have personal magnetism to a much greater degree than others?

A. That is always due to a sense of destiny, an inner knowledge of the soul. It generally means a greater "aliveness."

Q. What causes an arresting personality?

A. What I have said: a fuller and greater realization of the self, by which I mean the soul.

3

Pre-Natal State

⁓

I should like to say a few words about the pre-natal state, but it must be understood that what I say is theoretical: it is all given from hearsay. I have no absolute proof that it is true, but I have good reason to believe that I am right in these statements.

At the moment of conception the child becomes an individual soul. It may be that it has been in the world before, and in that case it has decided to reincarnate, on the other hand, it may be its first excursion. Heredity is the inheritance of the soul that makes its first adventure in the Universe. The reincarnated soul inherits nothing from the parents it has chosen.

Now I want to follow the child, who makes its first adventure, from the moment of its conception. The parents have created a physical body, but what of the soul? Where does the soul come from? What is its origin?

The Soul complete at the Moment of its Conception.

The soul of the unborn child is complete at the time of its conception. It has spent years on its own formation. Long before the marriage of the parents, the child's soul had come into being. For in time – that is, our time – there is no past, present or future, though we imagine there is: and the souls of these children had come into being with the horoscopes of the parents. It had been decided that the parents should come together, and give to the children's souls, houses to dwell in and to develop from.

Where the new soul originates we do not know; as I said in the last chapter we can only conjecture its source. We are told it descends into the physical. We do know that the soul was complete at the time of the child's conception. That part of it which I shall call the "Watcher" knew its fate, the fate that was irrevocably laid down for it, knew also its horoscope, and the periods in which the Watcher could possibly avert the dangers that threatened it. All through life on the Earth sphere, the Watcher keeps guard over the life of the soul, protects it as far as is possible, and at the hour of death enters more fully into its consciousness.

The "Watcher"

What is the "Watcher"? It is the fuller consciousness of the soul, to which it will arrive in the higher sphere to which it is on its way. It will carry a Watcher with it until the whole journey is accomplished. The Watcher is part of the soul itself: it has nothing to do with teachers, guides, or controls, and it is the guardian of the soul through the whole journey.

That is all I can say about the pre-natal state.

4

Reincarnation

~

Theosophical doctrines teach that every soul must return to the Earth sphere and live in the body in order that it may exhaust what is called its Karma or original sin. This is considered by Theosophists to be the only theory which accounts for the unevenness of the conditions in the Earth life. It is an absurd contention, for if it were so, it would seem that free will were non-existent, and that there was a supreme and cruel purpose behind that punished or rewarded us, at the cost of centuries of suffering, both mental and physical.

No, this is not the case. Those who reincarnate do so through their own desires, the decision comes from themselves. It may be that in some cases the Watcher of the soul thrusts it back into incarnation because he believes it will benefit by a second life, but it must not be imagined that reincarnation is forced on anybody.

I will not try to explain what "original sin" is, for candidly I do not know, but I shall try and explain under what circumstances a human soul can escape reincarnation.

The first question you ask is: does the larger proportion of souls who come over from the Earth sphere return to it? No, by far the larger proportion continue their development on our side, and do not enter the restriction of the physical body again.

The Souls who do not Return

Let us deal with those who do not return. It is most improbable that the soul who has no desire to return, will be obliged to do so. Its Watcher may force it for some special reason, but this is very rare. The uneven fates of those who are still on the Earth sphere is a problem which can be explained in many ways. Explanations differ in various cases, but I should say that, as a rule, things are evened up in the journey through the spheres. If the life has been very hard or very miserable on Earth, the soul will be happier in the same proportion in the next sphere. If it has spent life in an evil manner, it need not go back to the Earth, it can be held up in its course through the sphere above it, and cleanse itself through this delay. Those who spent the Earth life badly may desire to return, in fact they often do, but they cannot be forced to do so. They run the risk after death of being held in the web of the astral, but many are not caught in it.

Hungers Which Cannot be Gratified

They enter our sphere and remain in the lowest plane until they have lost the tendency to evil, having achieved this they rise and pass through the sphere more rapidly than the average individual. This is what we believe in my sphere, and you may well say that in the last case I speak of, there is no punishment or suffering for the evil doer. But you must understand that those who carry over coarse or lustful tastes into the spheres above them suffer from hungers which cannot be gratified, that those who suffer from evil or revengeful passions cannot allay them by slaying or injuring their fellow beings after they have gone from the Earth. They must wait on the lower planes until these tastes or passions have burnt themselves out.

24

Conditions in the Lower Planes

You ask about the lower planes: what are the conditions there: surely above the Earth there can be nothing that is not superior to Earth conditions? Yes, the place we are in is superior to the Earth, and it has much greater possibilities than the Earth sphere, but if you enter it trammelled by evil tendencies you have not the power to enjoy it nor the desire to expand. You are thrown into a condition which harasses you. You long to get back to the familiar, encompassing body. You are oppressed by the light and sound, yet you are too lethargic to return to the place from whence you came.

The inhabitants of these lower planes often complain of the darkness there, by this they mean mental and spiritual darkness, and not the ocular sensation you call light.

The larger number of evil doers who come over and escape the astral web remain a very long time in these low planes: then suddenly they develop and ascend rapidly.

They have rid themselves of nearly all the ballast that held them down, and therefore progress easily.

I want you to realize that those souls who are caught in the web of the astral plane suffer far more, and experience greater unhappiness, than those evil doers who dwell in lower planes. They generally succeed in getting back to the Earth after a long period of horrific and evil dreams. And always remember, that to them the dreams are "reality", but those who do manage to get back are in the minority. The difficulty in extracting a soul from the astral web is very great, for the astral web, is the state where there are no moral responsibilities, and these poor souls prey on, and torture each other. The astral web, though inevitably a temporary abode, is the worst fate that can befall the soul.

Return a Choice, not a Law

I have said that the majority do not return. That is true. In the mass, life does not desire to repeat an experience. In nature, you do not see repetition, until full development is attained, and it is so with the soul's development. There is an innate and subconscious desire to gain perfection, and a reluctance to retrace its footsteps. But there are exceptions and I will not deny for a moment, that those who believe in reincarnation are not to some extent justified. The mistake they make is, that they speak of return to Earth as a law, or necessity, whereas it is a matter of choice. The memories or recollections of vague lives before Earth life are no proof of reincarnation. They may be memories of former lives on the Earth, or, as is more often the case, they are pictures which are shown by the guides, and are visions of a far distant ancestry. This is the usual explanation of these vague and fleeting memories.

The only real proof that a soul has been on Earth before is a definite memory which begins with its death, and continues to its birth in the former incarnation. This does not occur often, but it has been known. In cases of this kind there is no doubt about there having been a previous life on Earth.

You must not confuse obsession with memory of previous incarnation. An obsessing entity can appear to give a memory of another Earth life, which is merely its own memory, and has nothing to do with the life of the soul it has thrown out.

Good and Evil

I will now attempt to give you my views on the question of the predominance of good or evil, in certain individuals. Every soul that is born into the world contains all potentialities of good and evil in itself. If it reverses the course of its being, if it lives on its evil parts, rather than on the parts of itself which are capable of expansion, all growth is impossible. The force of evil will always pull the soul downward towards its roots, while the force for good will push it upwards. Evil can be defined as the opponent of development. The desire to keep the soul from a full realization of itself is an evil desire. This cannot be treated as a personal matter. We know of no devil in the universe, but we do know that certain forces work for retrogression.

The Criminal

The criminal corrupts his power to grow. He just stays where he is, opening himself up to the forces of evil. He lives in his evil parts, and attracts evil towards him. When he dies he remains in a dream, or rather in a nightmare condition until the desire to grow returns to him, the desire to have another chance and to forget the past. This comes in time to all who have lived in their evil parts, and then they are born again, and often in the new incarnation they are extremely fine people.

When Evil Predominates

I will try and explain some of these cases. There is the person who is too indolent to use his higher powers, who finds it easier to open himself up to evil than to good. These are the worst cases, for evil works through them and increases. Then there are the weak ones who sink under the burden of growth, and let the evil winds blow them where they will.

These are not as criminal as the first class, they merely act as channels for evil. Then there are others who are so open, that though they may begin as ordinary individuals, they end by becoming a counterpart of their environments. Through their astrological aspect there is the natural tendency, for instance, in some to evil. Some are born under influences which give them little chance. With the enormous mass of life pressing into the world, some must be unfortunate. This seems unjust, but we cannot look for what you call justice at every stage of our journey.

The Astrological Aspect

All we can demand is that the soul will be fully developed at some stage. If it is incarnated on Earth at some unfortunate time, it will probably pass into the next sphere at a particularly fortunate time, and find itself benefited in the process. But let us hold on to the comforting assurance that all and each will eventually attain perfection.

Questions and Answers

Q. "Some must be unfortunate" – This doesn't seem just.

A. There is no injustice to any morsel of life which comes into the world. If there are uneven chances whilst on Earth, in the sphere above they will find things much better for them, than for others who have had an easier Earth journey. Justice is Justice when all is fulfilled, but it cannot be measured by your sense of justice on every plane.

Q. What happens to those who commit murder?

A. If the crime is caused through obsession, the man who has committed it, is set free through a special ritual, allowed to rest for a time, and then goes back to the world if he wishes to do so. Criminals of this type generally desire to return. But if the crime is committed for material gain, without obsession, and from sheer perverted love of cruelty and suffering, these people spend a long time in darkness. Not in our sphere, not in yours, but between the two – the astral web of dreams. The dreams such criminals have are nightmares. They return, not of their own free will, but because they must be remade.

Q. Does remorse after committing murder help?

A. Yes, in a sense it is wiped out, it is expiated. Part of the life force is taken from the murderer and given to the murdered. This means that the murderer's path is blocked. He cannot go forward until he has made expiations, he has to stand still on his spiritual road.

Q. What happens to intellectual criminals?

A. It depends. It is difficult to put them all into one class, in fact, it is impossible. If the intellectual side is highly developed, and there is a criminal tendency, the person is completely uneven. One half of his personality soars, while the other is face downwards. It has to be readjusted. The lower and evil half has to incarnate again, before any progress can be made.

Q. How do suicides fare?

A. That also is difficult to put under one heading. If the suicide is committed because pain cannot be endured, there is only the natural result of sudden death, a longer period of unconsciousness. But if the suicide has been committed to escape consequences, the memory of what has occurred can go on torturing the victim to an extent that may be compared with obsession. That may continue for years of your time. Eventually he will awake from the trance, realize that the thread of life was cut too soon, and will plunge back of his own accord into the Earth life again.

Q. If one commits suicide to make life easier for others?

A. That person would not suffer much. There would be a long period of confusion, but eventually he would continue his road like any normal being.

Q. What happens when obsession causes suicide?

A. Then the man is allowed to purify himself of the obsession. Then, when he is free, he is compelled as a rule to come back through his own desire to complete his life.

Q. What about monstrosities of the Jack-the-Ripper type?

A. These are badly made human beings, or in some cases, a double soul, an evil one having entered with the good one. It may be that the soul is weak and small, and allows itself to be a prey to an

29

evil influence that dominates it. That does not happen often, but occasionally, and this is the explanation of dual personality. All monstrosities, whether of the mind or of the body, should be regarded as incomplete articles turned out too hastily in the hurry of creation.

Q. What happens to these eventually?

A. The misshapen soul has to be divided again into the two parts of spirit and mind, and can be remade so that where there had been disharmony between these two, there would be perfect harmony. This would take time. The newly made soul might not return for several years. The reason these monstrosities occur is because the "parts" do not harmonize, they jangle. The soul in such a case as that of Jack-the-Ripper would go on to our world, and as I have explained, it would be remade so that the proportions of good and evil were more balanced.

Q. Do "parts" of the personality ever reincarnate separately?

A. It is extremely rare that "parts" or what is generally known as "split-offs" of the personality return to Earth: but it does occur. I will try to explain by taking Napoleon as an example. His passion for cruelty, and his faithlessness to friends – these we may take as the worst parts of his character. After passing over, he would not be able to rise to high planes in the spheres above, because of these passions being round him. If he returned as a whole, there would of necessity be another upheaval, and another series of disasters. A personality such as his would not desire to return, but it would desire to complete itself, so it would subdivide and permit the incomplete parts to return to Earth for development. These split-off personalities would not have long lives. They would complete themselves as quickly as possible and return to set the entire personality free as a whole. I should describe such cases as Napoleon's as "group personalities", for in reality they possess more than the mental strength of one soul.

Napoleon was a colossus who was so vast that he was unable to steer himself wisely through life. He was very unevenly developed. Parts of the colossus would return, probably in humble environment, while he as an ego, would be helped on his journey.

Q. Would the parts of Napoleon functioning on this Earth, resemble him in character?

A. No, they would be the parts that were suppressed when he was whole.

Q. Can a soul time its own incarnation?

A. No, it cannot, but it will be hastened by its desire to return. You need not, and do not always live out your full life on any of the spheres.

Q. Is it possible to delay the date of passing from this plane?

A. If an individual man has an overwhelming desire to remain longer on the Earth plane, that desire might, and sometimes does, push the date of his passing further on in time. This depends entirely upon the strength of the desire.

Q. Then the day of death is not determined?

A. It is true that the man is born with the day and manner of his death, but so strong is the force of desire that it is possible that the day may be postponed, but merely for a short time, and then part of the personality would have passed over to our sphere already. This would occur in the case of very old people.

Q. Can people advance the day of death?

A. Yes, again desire would push back the date. It would have to be concentrated desire. It is a very rare happening, but it does happen occasionally.

Q. Does the presence of a younger person enable an older person to live longer?

A. Yes, it can do so, but the old person would lead a feeble mental existence, and would have lost a good many characteristics of his personality.

Q. What about very old people passing over?

A. With old people the arrival is hardly worthy of the name, they have come over gradually, and are quite familiar with our side. They are somewhat in the position of an infant, because these people who are familiar with their surroundings (which of course the infant is not) are slowly accepting the new conditions and are taking them into their consciousness. Those who come to us in full vigour of manhood have a harder struggle and a longer period before they can say they begin to live.

Q. If they are so familiar with your side, why should so many old people have such a strong desire to remain here?

A. That is the fault of the body. The old body clings to the young soul and depends on it. This enters the subconscious mind.

Q. Are there sudden passings on through accident from your sphere to the next?

A. Yes, there can be too rapid development which shoots the soul forward before its time.

Q. Does it return – reincarnate?

A. Not necessarily, but it may.

Q. What happens in the case of supermen?

A. They can choose and select the body that can hold them. Having had the whole experience they leave nothing to chance. The reincarnation is deliberate.

Q. Do affinities progress together through the spheres?

A. Yes, of course they do. If they reincarnate, the last incarnation would come when they had full understanding of their relation to each other. After that they would travel on through the spheres until the two became one in reality.

Q. Can one affinity reincarnate and the other not?

A. It is possible for one of these affinities to go through the Earth-incarnation at a stage of lower development than the other. That condition would mean the lesser developed of the two would not fully recognize the other, and in that case the lesser developed would probably reincarnate, while the other would remain on the sphere immediately above the Earth until the two were equalized and united, when they would continue their journey together.

Q. Can souls reincarnate in groups?

A. No, certainly not. It is impossible: remember I use the word "impossible" for a group of persons to time their re-appearance on the Earth sphere.

Q. Is there a reason for some passing over through accidents?

A. Planetary influences. A man is born with the day of his death decided, and even the manner of his death.

Q. Then if one is to be killed – say, run over by a motorbus – that cannot be avoided?

A. An accident would be in his horoscope. I was born with shipwreck and drowning, for instance.

Q. Had your father some subconscious knowledge of this? He was always so fearful of letting you go on the water, and yet never minded your playing with gunpowder?

A. Yes, he knew subconsciously that it was dangerous for me.

Q. Would a warning have averted it?

A. Not in my case. I was bound to go. Psychic warnings are given when there is a chance of injury which can be averted, not when there is a certainty of death.

Q. Do the souls clothed in deformed bodies reincarnate?

A. These people often do reincarnate, but if they have borne their trouble patiently, and have developed the soul, they need not return.

5

Life after Death

~

First Experiences

For a brief period of time after the soul has discarded the body it comes into the full realization of itself, but it is only momentary. It misses the constriction of the body. It is appalled by its own extent and size.

Its consciousness is confused for a long time, for now it has come to the point where it has to choose its next life. In order to do this, it has to make a tremendous effort. It must endeavour to function as a whole. The choice is not involuntary, it is aware of its own responsibility. It recognizes its own powers acquired through its Earth life, and in view of them has to choose where it will function.

In what place does it find itself? Between two worlds perhaps, you think. No: it is conscious of two worlds or two states: the state it left, and the state where it is to go. It sees itself as a whole for a short time in fact. It is a bewildering experience. If wise, it escapes from this distressing condition and, with its Earth memories, creates an illusion for itself, so that this part of it is lulled into rest. The word "death" means little to it now; it cannot decide whether the severance has taken place, as it finds life continuous.

Plane of Delirium, This condition is what the Theosophists have described as the astral plane. In a sense it is a plane, but "astral" does not describe it so well as the plane of "delirium". This is the only word I can think of that gives you any idea of the complete upheaval that occurs after death. The actual moment of passing releases the soul into a mirage. It can no longer tell what is real and what is unreal. What it is most fully conscious of, is its own utter helplessness and want of purpose. This state does not last very long unless the manner of dying has been injurious to the soul. If the thread of life has been suddenly severed, it leaves a wound which would not occur if the passing had been gradual.

Experience of "The Blue Island" Necessary

You will ask me: " What about The Blue Island? " I have already said it was a dream, or an illusion.

Being versed in what I might expect after death, I knew instinctively that in order to get over the period of delirium quietly and without suffering, I must create a dream for myself and the others. Capture some of the memories that were storming through me in confusion, and mould them into a world of fancy. This I did, and I lived through that period in The Blue Island with them. My father met me: he was quite real. I saw him as he came in and out, and knew that he was taking part in my dream. The Blue Island lasted many days, but when I communicated I was quite out of it, quite clear. I will try to explain.

After I left my body, after I realized that we were all drowned and that the ship had gone down, I knew I must do something for the living, and for the dead. With one part of myself I returned and communicated: with another part I told those who were with me the story I told you in *The Blue Island*, and all those who listened were actually there for this period of confusion. When the story was finished they were safe in their own homes beginning their new lives.

Now I must explain that the period of delusion or dream varies with the individual. Some people have a much shorter period than others, but it occurs in all cases. Now and then in isolated cases the part which communicates with the Earth is clear. It was so in my case. I was not confused after I had dived into the Earth atmosphere. Although another part of me had deliberately created a tale, a dream for itself, the part that returned to Earth was quite conscious of the past, and of all that had happened.

Free from the Cramp of the Body

The only bewildering thing was, that space offered no difficulty. I could travel over the Earth almost instantaneously. This seemed strange as I broadcasted my messages, and yet I was not distressed by it. I realized that what was called death had taken place, that I was suddenly set free from the cramp of the body, which had confined me like a cage.

Time Non-Existent

So I did my work, and in doing it, I did not take time into consideration. Soon I realized that time did not exist any more, which is a concept impossible to the Earth mind. It was true, however, time seemed to poise or to rush backward or forward. The past seemed one with the present and future. Few persons are likely to have my experience, for in my case I had so prepared myself for the change, and felt myself on the threshold of it so often, that it did not surprise or alarm me. I can say quite sincerely, that fear kept outside me. It never entered into my thoughts, but I cannot promise that it would be so in all cases.

Then I wondered why it was, that my conscious mind seemed to reach from the dream of The Blue Island to the Earth, from the Earth to The Blue Island.

It was difficult to decide where one state of consciousness ended and the other began. I did not feel that I was alone. I was everywhere, with everyone I loved and knew at the same moment. The people of The Blue Island seemed quite concrete, absolutely human.

They talked, they answered questions. I saw them move and eat and drink. With the people on the Earth the experience was similar, but they looked different from the inhabitants of The Blue Island, they seemed to glow. I could see the inner body shine like a light through the outer. I could see them as I should see the lights of a town, if I were in an aeroplane above it. I shall pass over this period, perhaps returning to it later on.

Life in the Full Sense

I shall now try to describe the sensation when The Blue Island slowly disappeared, and life in the full sense began. It was the most emotional experience of my existence so far. Birth may have some resemblance to it, but the infant consciousness differs so much from the consciousness of an adult that we can only guess what its sensations are. I may say that I felt neither an infant nor an old man when consciousness knit itself together again. I felt I was young and vigorous, but no child. The first sensation was a joyous movement. I had the shape of a man, the sensation of strength, and the power to use my limbs freely.

Clothed, – but How?

I looked at my garments, for I had garments which seemed quite appropriate and natural. I was not familiar with the material they were made of. It felt extraordinarily light, and had a web-like quality, which no cloth I could remember possessed. It was coloured, too, the colour subdued, not brilliant, but definite. It seemed to me to be blue.

I was quite sure that life had begun in earnest, because I was now able to shut off my consciousness of the life on Earth, and was living fully on my own sphere.

The House I had Prepared

I noticed the house I was in seemed familiar. Surely I had planned it, and had built it as I wished. I knew all its corners and crannies, and certain shelves for my books which I myself had specially designed. I had travelled over it in sleep hundreds and hundreds of times. I understood it now. I had grown up on the sphere I was on, just as I had grown up on the Earth sphere: and when I had come to years of discretion I had prepared a house for my home-coming, had chosen it, planned it, had been there thousands of hours perhaps. I realized this because my conscious mind had expanded. There was a wider field for memory now.

I sat down and looked out of the window at the landscape. I had chosen quite a beautiful spot for my house. It was close to a wood. There was a garden outside with brilliant flowers. I remember planting them, and it did not surprise me to see a flame in the heart of each of these blossoms. It looked like a flame: it was white and enhanced the colour of the flower that cupped it. This seemed quite natural, and I wondered why I had never noticed it before.

Here I must cut off the record of these sensations, and try to recall, how far my memory of the Earth functioned at this time. It was far more definite than it had been when I was on the Earth plane.

Memories of my Earth Life

When I was there, pressure of business and, later on, age made it difficult to single out and select memories from the past, but now I could see the past with a magnifying glass, and see it as a whole. How small it looked! I said to myself: "I talked of years and a lifetime when I was there, and now it seems like a moment." Then came the thought – what about the future? I looked around the room. No one was there. There was a great stillness in the house. I wondered why I was by myself at such a moment.

Then a great wave of emotion overwhelmed me. I felt for the moment all the joys and grief of a lifetime. I knew that I had lost nothing, that all the emotions were alive, and that I was left alone to enjoy and suffer this unique experience.

Every soul must suffer and enjoy as I did. When memory of emotion comes back like a tide, the soul is swamped for a moment until the wave passes, and it returns to a sense of calm and balance.

After that I felt even more alive than before, and I thought I would go and talk to my parents. I knew quite well where they lived. I could be there in a moment and could share the experience I had just had with them. Happiness, joy had returned. I had no sense of loss. I held all the past in me: the future stretched ahead. I could almost see it, or perhaps it would be better to say I could "feel" it.

I visit my Parents

I went to see my father and mother and I heard a lot about The Blue Island from them. My father congratulated me warmly. He said he wished he had had my knowledge when he came over. He spent a long time in foolish and futile dreams which helped nobody. My mother's experience was different. She said she had slept peacefully after her death. She had no memory, until she woke up, and found herself at home in the care of her own mother.

Tracing by means of Personal Vibrations

When I came back to my own house, the question arose, what was I going to do next? I realized that my first duty was to the inhabitants of The Blue Island, who must still be in my sphere, even if they were not on my plane. I must find them all.

This was a very difficult task, for I had no knowledge of the use of personal vibrations at that time, but with my father's help I was able to trace one by one my fellow passengers on the *Titanic*.

I can now trace any individual I wish, either in my own sphere, or on Earth, by his, or her vibration, but at that early period of my career I had no idea how I could differentiate between one vibration and another.

This I had to learn, and I was not able to teach myself. It worried me a little to feel so stupid about this, so there was nothing for it but to go back to my father's house, and consult him about it. He laughed a good deal at my question. He said, "If you want to communicate with people in your own sphere, visualize them, that will give you the vibration, and you will be able to trace them in a moment. If you want to discover people on Earth, there are two methods. If they think of you intensely you will see them. If you want them yourself, and they are not thinking of you, visualize them, and they will receive the impression in some way. This will give you a vibration by which you can trace them."

How the Tracing is done

In order to give you some idea of how this is achieved, I must refer to television which is, as you know, the conversion of a sound into an image. Suppose my friend A. is on Earth. I lost sight of him years ago, and want to find him. How shall I set about it? Firstly I become passive and visualize my memory of him as vividly as I can. This causes a sound, and that sound has the power to summon. I come into his thoughts at once, and through that thought, which reacts to mine, I can trace him without difficulty and reach him in a moment.

The same applies to my own sphere when I want to find anyone. It is not so easy as it sounds, and it was not easily achieved. I had a long training before I could be sure of the result. Here I may as well say that in our sphere this power of reading personal vibration does not help us with the sphere above us.

Those who have passed on there have the power to find us when they desire to do so, but they are shut away from us, except during sleep, when we can travel over to them.

We preserve our Shape and Appearance

I shall not digress now, except to say that after we pass the Earth barrier, and enter the extension of the Earth, which is where I am

41

now, senses are given us which we do not possess before that time. I wish to be emphatic on this point, we preserve our shape and appearance, otherwise our vibration would mean nothing. Those who imagine us as nebulae are mistaken, because, although it is possible to dematerialize the soul body, that state is not natural, and when it is in that condition, it would not strike its own vibration, which is necessary for its tracing by other souls.

Difference in vibration of Embodied and Disembodied

Another question is: how can we on our side find and identify others who may be on, not higher but other planes and spheres, and who have passed on before us? That again is a matter of vibration, but before I explain this, I should like to say that the vibration of a disembodied soul, and the vibration of a soul still encased in the body, is very different. The vibration of a soul still in the body is dull, it is not sharp.

If I had no idea whatever as to who my communicator was, I could tell by the vibration whether he were alive or dead. As a matter of fact, it is far easier to trace people on our side than on yours, and even those on higher planes than our own, although we cannot actually reach these higher spheres without the aid of a medium. In the spheres beyond ours it is possible to trace individual souls just as we trace them in my sphere, but we cannot get vibrations from the actual spheres above our own. So that question is answered. Television goes far to explain it, for when you reflect that each of us, has not only his own sound, but his own image contained in the sound, it is not so difficult to imagine what happens here, without any instrument or apparatus.

42

6

WHAT HAPPENS AT DEATH

~

Now let us return to the moment of death, and analyse what happens. Let us take first, a case where the passage has been partly accomplished before the soul is severed from the body, as in long illness or old age, and secondly let us take a case of sudden death, in youth preferably, and analyse it.

Death through Sickness

The vibration of a soul in the body is, as I have said, dull compared with that of a disembodied soul.

When the body is sick, it becomes duller still, unless the patient is unconscious, and the soul leaves the body.

The sick man's vibrations are very weak, and we can tell the exact state of his health, from the image we have of him. When he was well, his image seemed illuminated, but now that he is ill, it fades, there is little or no light there. We see it becoming dimmer and dimmer as the illness progresses. Now he becomes unconscious, and we know that the soul is free, almost as it would be in healthy sleep, but not quite so. Let me explain. In sleep the soul escapes from the body. The cord is elastic, and in some cases the soul can travel to

43

high planes and spheres, and return to the body in the fraction of a second. Now in illness this is not the case. The soul leaves the body slowly. The cord is dull and stretches with difficulty.

The soul hangs over the physical body. You have probably seen photographs of this condition. Now the moment of death is at hand. We have prepared for this, we who are the friends and relatives of the dying man. He sees us from the moment he leaves the body, before the cord is severed, but his senses are dulled. He may not recognize us, or he may regard us as a dream. Now the cord has withered completely, it falls back into the physical body and the soul is free. We receive it into our care

I want to make this explanation as clear as possible, so that my readers may understand the strange conditions they will be sure to encounter when they pass over.

The soul is freed, and for a few moments – the time varies with different individuals – it becomes intensely conscious, chiefly of the people it has left behind on Earth. It visualizes them so distinctly that it can, and often does, appear to them, even if they are at a great distance.

Now we who are the friends of the dead man have him in our care, and he is rapidly ascending into our realms of consciousness away from the Earth, but his imagination is so vivid, he has conjured up so definite a picture of certain persons left behind, that he is able to see and speak to them with a projection of his conscious mind. Fortunately this state does not last long.

The consciousness contracts again, and soon he is completely with his friends on our side, gathering together as it were the rags of his consciousness: because, just for this one fraction of these few moments after death, the soul is scattered, it is not a coherent unit.

Sudden Death

Now shall we take the case of sudden death. A young man of twenty has been run over in the street and killed. He has died instantly. How does the snapping of the healthy cord of life affect him? The soul leaves the body with a leap. It finds itself free.

His friends may or may not have been ready to receive it. It may again have a moment of vivid consciousness, but it seldom has unless the possibility of death has been in the mind beforehand, as occurs in war, for instance. Then the soul begins its ascent into a higher realm of consciousness at once, otherwise in cases of sudden death, whether it is alone or accompanied, it fails to collect itself; it strays about in patches, as it were, for quite a long time, during which the conscious mind does not function in the least. The whole being is a nebulae of vague fancies.

Then the soul gradually contracts. This takes place very slowly, it may take months. The consciousness returns gradually. One day the young man wakes up amongst his friends and asks what has happened. In such cases the soul would have no memory of its passing, and would not recognize the fact that he had died. The news has to be broken to him.

You may ask, was this my case after the shipwreck? I have already told you. No, it was not: but remember that I was prepared, and for a little while before we sank we knew that we were in danger, so the possibility of death had entered our conscious minds.

Consciousness: What is it?

"Consciousness." I have used the word very glibly, but what do I mean by it? This, that while you are on the Earth, you use a certain portion of yourself for your daily needs, for all your loves and hates, for all your adventures. All your joys and sorrows are felt by only a part of you which I call the consciousness.

When the conscious mind is out of action, the whole being is in chaos. The dam does not hold the water back any longer: it flows through. The human being is not able to function with the whole of itself, until it reaches a very advanced stage in its existence.

I have explained, feebly perhaps, but as well as I can, what happens at the moment of death, and I shall not return to this subject again. But before I leave it, I shall go back to birth, for the entry of a soul into the world is as important as its leave-taking.

Comparison between the Newly Born and the Newly Dead

It may be asked, what is the consciousness of an infant? Does it function in an infinitesimally small part of itself? No, that is not so. The infant is possessed of as much use of the conscious mind as the adult, but it uses it in a different manner. It compresses it, so that it merely functions for its actual needs. The conscious mind of the child at birth is as vivid as the conscious mind of the mother: but the intellect of the child has not been called into play.

That is, it has not yet begun to sort out and arrange its sensations. So the infant and the newly departed are in exactly the same position. The difference that actually exists between the newly born, and the newly dead, is that the newly dead suddenly begin to use their intellectual power. It comes into play in a moment, whereas the infant arrives at the same point slowly.

Our Next Great Move

We have now finished with the moment of death.

We have spoken of the moment of birth, and I have tried also, to give you some idea of how life begins in a new sphere.

Let us take a leap and, for the moment, pass on to the next great move in our existence. I mean the move towards the sphere above the one on which I am now. Of this I can only speak from study and hearsay.

I do not like the word "death" I would like to erase it from all languages, but in this connection it applies almost as it applies on the Earth sphere. When we pass from our sphere to the one above, it means again a change in consciousness, an extension of the mind, and in order to arrive at this, there must be a pause and a break. There is no suffering, bodily or mental, in our passage from one sphere to another, once the break is made. Preparation for the break causes no anxiety or alarm.

A Pause and a Break

When we pass on to the next sphere we are unconscious, for a time which varies according to the individual. The time which is most usual is what you would call the space of about one year. Sometimes it is longer. The soul slips into a state of coma, breaks its bonds like a butterfly, and soars up into the new life.

The Joy of Life

The joy of life increases with the rate of vibration. There is no sin that exceeds the sin of losing enjoyment in the actual act of living. The further the soul rises the more it loves life. This seems to cast aspersion on the early Christian ideals of suffering as Christ suffered. It is not so in reality, for suffering such as Christ's contains all that is the essence of joy and pain together, the pair of opposites.

Thus an ideal is put forward for us, the ideal of living in the fullest sense of the word, of sucking every morsel of sweetness from what we are given.

We have the assurance of ever-increasing life, and consequently ever-increasing joy. We should never forget this: nor should we weep for those who have passed on before us, for they have attained greater life than we can possess where we are.

Questions and Answers

Q. What happens when an individual passes on alone, not in a group as in the case of the *Titanic* victims?

A. As a rule, confusion and distorted dreams for quite a long time, if the death has been sudden.

Q. Did only a part of your consciousness function when you were on The Blue Island?

A. Yes, but in the case of The Blue Island I was aware that we had to pass through the stage of scattered personality, and I deliberately wove a dream world out of a mixture of my consciousness and intellectual part.

Q. Did the others understand?

A. No, they did not, nor did I think it wise to enlighten them. Many of them had never thought about the problems of life and death. I let them live their dream life in peace.

7

Our Life Here

~

I am anxious to reply, as far as I can, to the natural questions which everyone must ask about our life here. I shall answer these questions to the best of my ability, with the hope that my readers will understand that I am dealing with a different dimension where first, the rate of the life-vibration is twice as rapid as on the Earth, secondly, our world, though composed of the same material as yours, is less solid. The particles in it are more widely apart than in your world, and yet to us it appears more solid than your world does to you.

Differences that make exact Information difficult

In the same way, the physical body is more compact and heavier than the body we wear when we pass out of the Earth life. Yet to us, all the senses are much more acute that yours are to you. We see and hear more. Our sense of smell is more delicate. Our emotions respond more quickly. All this rapid rate of life, it must be remembered, means that time is different for us: that which seems a year to you would seem much less than a year to us. Thus it is difficult for us to calculate time as you know it on Earth. Now I shall take these simple questions in rotation.

1. Do We Eat?

Yes, certainly we do. Our bodies must have nourishment, just as yours must, but our food is less solid than yours. For instance, we do not eat the flesh of animals, nor do we eat cooked foods. Our nourishment comes from the vegetable growths here, and certain materials which we get from the ether, which would be the equivalent of wine or tea to you, stimulants when we are tired or exhausted. This food comes off as a vapour from our bodies, that is, the unnecessary part, but there is little that is not necessary for our existence.

2. Are We Clothed?

When the spirit leaves the body in sleep, and enters our sphere temporarily, it clothes itself with the ectoplasmic vapour that it draws from the body. When the spirit leaves the body permanently, it carries with it clothing from the same source as that which it drew from when it made its temporary excursions in sleep. This clothing, however, is not permanent, it decays and withers very soon. When the spirit recognizes the necessity for clothing, it decides what it requires, and receives it, as it receives its material for its house, from the ether, but it must have the actual clothes it needs in its mind.

3. Does Each Prepare His Own Dwelling?

Everyone who has any intelligence or wisdom builds a house. No one can design your house but yourself. You must see and imagine the house you want. You can be assisted and advised in your design. If your imagination cannot deal with the clothes you want, you can have skilled assistance for this also. You ask, is there any form of payment for this assistance? Yes, payment not in money, but in service. For instance, if someone helps you with your clothes, you pay for this help possibly in some form of suggestion, for which your knowledge gives you the facility.

There are a few, however, who build no houses. These paupers are taken into special asylums. By paupers, I mean people who in their Earth lives, have merely lived, eaten and drunk, and have never used the thinking apparatus that was given them. These have to begin again at the bottom rung of the ladder. Incomplete though this may seem, this is the best explanation I can give.

4. Do We Sleep?

Yes, of course. How, otherwise, could we become acquainted with the spheres above us. We sleep, for what would seem to you, an absurdly long time, but it is only a short time to us. We do not sleep every night, as you understand nights, day and night do not alternate here as yours do. Calculated by your time, we sleep every other night.

5. Are Professions Carried On?

Of course we carry on our work, the work we have done in our Earth life, unless it relates to money or merchandise. The vast number who come to us, who have been occupied in finance or business, are unemployed at first, because our system of exchange is different from that to which they have been accustomed on Earth. They have to learn our system, and that means education. But employment is found for them very quickly. When I say we find work for them, I do not mean that a staff of warders looks after them. I want to dispel the mistaken idea that we are forced to do this and that. Their first task is common to all who pass over: as soon as possible they must help their brethren who have passed more recently than they have. This occurs automatically just as in a battle, the wounded who are conscious would try to help those who are more seriously wounded. After that time of probation is over, they will have had enough experience to begin life in our schools and hospitals. We always have room for numbers of newcomers in these vast places.

Medicine

Medicine is studied with great keenness in our sphere, not only with a view to helping those on Earth, but for treatment of those who are on our own sphere.

We have forms of illness peculiar to ourselves, of which I will speak later on.

The workers who help researchers on Earth are a separate body from our own medical men.

Law

Application of law is continued here. Our barristers and judges have a different sense of justice from yours. They are occupied first in the study, and later in the administration of our laws. That profession continues almost without interruption.

The Army

Yes, the Army and Navy have their own work here, not to encourage war, but to further a general peace, both here and in your world. All your peace congresses are ruled from our sphere.

Science

There is no cessation in science. Research has every advantage on our sphere. Again, research is advanced not only on the Earth sphere, but on our own. We have our chemists and astronomers, our engineers, both practical and theoretical. We have our architects, too. All forms of art continue, and are closely linked up with religion, for perfection can be attained through any form of art, and the true artist here is looked upon as a priest who cannot teach the work he practises, except through inspiration and intuition.

The Arts

Music is the highest and the most inspirational of all the arts. It is necessary to us, for reasons of health, therefore almost everyone identifies himself with it, up to a point. Later on I shall speak more fully of this. Painting is enjoyed more widely than on your sphere, but the work is on less material lines. Writing is a most important profession, and our libraries are vast. We convey ideas without the use of words, by a process akin to your shorthand. We have sculptors, too, all the arts, in fact, are practised. The art of the Theatre is considered to be as important as any other. It takes the form of a vast school. There are groups who form themselves for the sole purpose of teaching through the art of the stage.

These subjects are far too vast to be spoken of here as replies to questions. I shall devote a whole chapter to the Arts, and another to the Professions.

6. Are We Conscious of Two Spheres at Once?

Almost everyone leads a life on two spheres at once. Some who are bad sleepers know little of the sphere above them, but most of us travel to the sphere above us in sleep, and there prepare the place we desire to live in. The place I had prepared was quite familiar to me, and I remember certain little details about which I had fidgeted a lot, but which I found were exactly as I had expected.

7. What Qualities in the Earth-Life Lead to Most Rapid Progression on Our Side?

That is a most important question, and in order to make my reply to that, clear to you, I must give you a diagram. Think of a spider's web in which the centre is closely woven, from which threads stretch out in all directions. Now the manner in which self-perfection can be attained may be by any of the threads which lead to the centre. This is a general statement, and I must define the word spirituality.

To be spiritual you must have trodden down the coarser and heavier parts of your nature to such an extent that you have practically forgotten them. You may do this through a love of your fellows: through religious ecstasy: through a desire to be perfect in any form of art: through courage: through any kind of work which you can do with all your might, and for the glory of God: through honesty in industry: through pity: and through the bearing of pain for yourself or others without complaint. All these things build a house worth living in on the other side. But let me extend a little. A sense of value is necessary for the accomplishment of anything that is worthwhile. He who accepts the values that are merely conventional, and is too indolent to search his own soul and find the right values, cannot go far on the spiritual road.

Essential Spiritual Values

Let me give an instance of what I mean. A mother has a child whom she adores. She gives him what she calls a mother's love, she cannot bear to let the child out of her sight. The child forms other ties which infuriate the mother, she pleads, is angry. The child is hurt, and begins to question himself as to whether it is right that these new influences have come into his life. That mother has a wrong sense of values.

What is Prayer?

I have told you of that which leads to a high spiritual life on our side, but I will add a sentence. Prayer is the concentration of desire, and only prayer in this sense is granted. Spirituality is a concentrated desire for perfection in any form of activity, a desire to do what has to be done as well and as perfectly as possible. I hope you see my point of view, for it is an all-important one.

8. Can I Define "Help"?

Help is the consideration of another's position. In order to help anyone, you must get into the skin of that person, look through his eyes, and feel what he feels. You must bring a sense of values to bear on the help you give. It would not help a spendthrift to give him a cheque for two hundred pounds. It would not help a sick person if you were continually condoling with him.

Help must be given with intelligence. Frequently the best way to help is to be sympathetic with the other's position, to let him talk, and imagine yourself in the situation he is in. This sounds easy, but as a matter of fact it is very difficult. Then having faced this position, you must consider whether he should solve his own problems, or whether it is wise for you to solve them for him. Never rob anyone of the birthright of his own responsibilities.

9. Do Those of Low Development on Earth Survive on Our Side?

It depends. The congenital idiot does not survive. He is put back into the melting-pot. In these cases the perfect union of soul and body has not taken place.

When the two cells unite to form a human being, life, which is the soul, enters it. If the cells have not united perfectly the whole construction goes wrong.

The soul is not destroyed but it lacks the power of development. It is endeavouring to function through an imperfect machine which must be renewed before progress can be effected.

10. How Do We Travel?

This is the most difficult question I have been asked, because we live at a rate of vibration which is quite incredible to you. But I must make an attempt to reply, though at best my explanation may be clumsy, and must not be taken too literally.

Think of the fastest machine you have, let us take your fastest aeroplane, even then you have not arrived at our rate of vibration, let us start from London and travel to Paris in it. This will take about a third of the time in which we could do the journey by train and boat. We shall have accomplished what would at one time have been considered a miracle. But here our rate of vibration is much more rapid even than an aeroplane, so if we started from London we could be in Paris in a fraction of a minute, less as a matter of fact, about ten seconds.

We use no locomotives of any kind, but we do use aeroplanes. All the machines we have are machines that travel by air, but these are only used for amusement. In the ordinary way we can cover ground as rapidly as thought can cover it. If we wish to go from one place to another, we are there.

Capacity for Travelling through Space

Whilst I am writing on this subject, I should like to tell you of our capacity, when developed, for travelling through space: that is going right out of one universe into another. We do this by a projection of the mind. We travel, yet we don't travel. It is difficult to give the idea. We are able to send out what is like a thread – there is no other word – that travels all over the invisible substance that scientists sometimes call the ether. It is something like a telephone wire, but we use it differently, in that a section of ourselves may travel along it if we wish to get outside of this particular universe. This is true, incredible though it may seem.

When we approach the Earth, or anything that is composed of matter, we enter into a subjective state.

We are not quite normal. This state corresponds in a way to a dreamer's state on Earth, but we have much more control of the condition. In this state we can go further than the stars you see. We pass right out of one universe into another, and we see what appears to your astronomers as nebulae. In other words, another universe – a universe containing myriads of other stars also.

Questions and Answers

Q. With reference to bad sleepers, surely some who are very bad sleepers are living good lives and must be preparing a home on the other side?

A. At some period of their existence they must have slept well, further, they sleep better than they imagine. There are very few really bad sleepers. Human beings can get into a condition in which their Earth consciousness is slightly active, and yet they are in our sphere.

Q. What happens to the souls who go over during sleep?

A. All of them work here. They have to become familiar with the conditions on our side, and naturally they are eager to learn. Tired people do not come to us at night. The people who visit us are in a sound healthy sleep, and though the body may be tired and resting, the soul is in full vigour when it breaks the bonds of the body and comes to us.

Q. Do we remember our life here, when over on your side during sleep?

A. Yes, certainly you do, and that is the part that saddens some of you when you have to go, when the curtain drops, and you are pulled back into the body with the knowledge that memory will not go back with you, this causes you poignant grief.

Q. What about wicked people who sleep well?

A. They pass on to their fellows on lower planes. They do not develop a desire for virtue at once, but they see people like themselves, who have realized the folly of their ways, and it helps them.

Q. What happens to good dull people?

A. They are not on the low planes, nor on very high planes either. They are the commonest cases of reincarnation. They realize their limitations gradually when they come here, and they want to go back to the world and dig up the talents they buried in the ground.

8

Arts and Professions

~

re most professions practised in our world? That is a question which everyone will desire to have answered. It would be disastrous if we found ourselves in new surroundings in a new world, with the knowledge we acquired in the old as useless as a suit of clothes. If this were so, there would seem to be no plan or scheme in existence.

When I speak of professions, I class them under two headings: those which require knowledge of a strictly business and commercial character, and those which are more highly intellectualized. To illustrate what I mean, I will give a specimen list of each.

1. Commercial Professions

I will take the commercial professions first. The Stock Exchange is a strictly commercial profession. It requires courage and intelligence, but it does not need severe intellectual training. Again, the solicitor, though his business is a very arduous and important one, is not comparable with the barrister who has to acquire the art of logical argument through a long and highly specialized training.

Although the banker cannot be said to require an intellectual training, yet he is a highly cultivated person in his own line, and it is not conceivable that his knowledge should be useless or a misfit in the world to which he is on his way.

All these I call commercial professions. Besides these, there are endless kinds of commerce from shipping downwards. All these forms of activity find a place on our side of life though their business may not be carried on in exactly the same way.

Money

This leads up to the question: is money still to torture us when we pass into the next sphere? No, there is no money here as there is in your world, but there is wealth of possession which always implies that the owner has earned it.

Poverty drives people into the lower planes of our sphere. What we call poverty is indolence, having the interest centred in the ego, and so on. It is not poverty in your sense of the word, for remember that no one is poor here so far as necessity goes. The poor on our side are on the lower planes of our sphere, as I said, but don't regard this as punishment. Regard it rather as planting the right seeds in the right place. I will not go further into the commercial professions. I have indicated roughly that work is found for those who follow them on our side, and nothing they have done on Earth is wasted. I will pass on to the more highly specialized professions.

2. Specialized Professions

The Army continues its work here, and so does the Navy. On our side, we influence the work on the Earth sphere. So far as we are concerned, our Army is organized for the purpose of preventing wars. It is composed of large bodies and councils of those who have served in wars on Earth, and so with the Navy also.

At present there is a great consolidated move on our side for peace on Earth. We have not done much so far with your peace councils, but we shall do more, we shall push against the war instinct in your world, until war is impossible. To you there seems a general chaos in the world, but you must understand that, in order to arrive at better things, the old conditions must be broken up, otherwise there could be no hope of change. This applies to the peace councils. They have not done much work so far, by which I mean they have done nothing that can eradicate war, but they are keeping war down, they are preventing a general upheaval.

The Church

We use our clergy, but they stand higher, and see more than they did when they were on Earth. Some go back into the melting pot. Some sink to low planes, but the finest of our clergy take high places on our side, and continue to teach and preach. Our religions here are as thoroughly organized as yours are.

Barristers and Judges

All our great barristers and judges, if they have been upright and honest according to their lights, continue their work on our side. We have our laws, and our legal men improve them and construct schemes for carrying them out. A barrister has not wasted his time on Earth. Then there are the dons, the professors and fellows in the Universities, the scientists, the classical and mathematical scholars, the literary men. All these are useful to us as they are to you. They continue with their work, as the schoolmasters do, with wider views and more enlightenment.

The Artists

The artists, including musicians and poets, are the happiest people who pass on to us. The sudden realization of clearer understanding of art and life is pure joy to them. They are our busiest people, and they radiate gladness. I must not forget to mention our actors, for theatres are as popular a form of art and amusement here as with you, and they, too, carry on their profession.

Music, however, has a wider field here than any of the other arts. It is used for healing purposes, as colour is also. Everyone on our side is a musician to a certain degree. Almost at once the need for music is felt, as hunger would be felt by you. The combination of harmony, rhythm and colour is our chief medical treatment, for we have our disorders here. We do not escape from all forms of illness, as many on Earth appear to think. I will presently write a whole chapter on medicine and nursing on our side, and will explain some of our treatments, but here let me include medicine among the professions which continue on our side. It is a most important profession, and one which cannot be taken too seriously by the doctors who are on the Earth, and who are dealing not only with the body but with the mind.

I must explain here that all the professions I have mentioned are practised on slightly different lines here, with the exception of the artists. We have to alter and modify the work of our soldiers, and sailors, our clergy and doctors.

All working in a wider Consciousness

They have all to add much to what they knew in your world, for always bear in mind that here, they are working in a wider consciousness.

You have now some conception of our world, I hope. You cannot possibly understand, what it is to live on a higher vibration, but you can see that there has been no waste, that what perhaps seemed drudgery on Earth was working towards an end, and that death – or what you call death – merely means a greater life.

Questions and Answers

Q. Are there some on your side who influence the world for war?

A. Certainly there are, but not on the higher planes. Those who believe in war are undeveloped, and will probably go back and fight it out on Earth.

Q. Are there various religions?

A. Yes, of course there are. People cannot leave the Earth plane with a firm belief and then suddenly lose it on our side. All forms of religion continue here, but there is less dogma. Those who do not belong to a special faith are not condemned by the others, that is the main difference.

Q. Do dogma and religion fall away as progress is made?

A. Yes, they do, but not on our sphere, or even on the one above it. Definite religious opinions hold good until we are half way through our journey.

Q. Is there a special Christ sphere?

A. Well, that is difficult to answer. Christ exists now in the faith He diffused on Earth, and all who call themselves Christians have the opportunity to worship him here, and even at some of our services he may appear symbolically. As a personality we do not meet Him, nor is there any special sphere His. He is diffused through all the spheres.

Q. Julia speaks of the "Christ sphere."[2]

A. Julia adapts herself to the understanding of those she is teaching, and literally speaking, any sphere might be called the " Christ sphere."

---

[2] See *After Death: Letters From Julia*, W. T. Stead. (White Crow Books, 2011.)

Q. She speaks of meeting him.

A. She would see him at our services, where people are gathered together for prayer and worship. He may appear amongst them as he did after his resurrection: by which I mean, he may have the quality of a vision, a vivid one no doubt, but it is different from a physical presence.

9

Medicine and Nursing

~

As I have already told you we have our disorders. My dear friends, did you expect to pass from your world to ours, and to lose every form of trouble and illness? Do you seriously believe you deserve to pass, from what is generally called a world of sorrow, and enter a paradise where all is happiness?

Our Sick

It is true that our disorders are not physical like yours, but most of you have felt pain of the mind. Mental pain is what we suffer here. Let us first discuss our medical equipment. We have large hospitals where our disorders are treated. We have nurses and doctors to look after our sick. I expect the first question that is on your lips is: what do the doctors do in our world? Do they treat disorders in the world to which they have passed, or do they work for the benefit of those who are still in the world they have left? Both. Some devote themselves to illnesses of the body only. These naturally, must find their work on the Earth sphere, but there are those who give all their time to our ailments on the sphere in which I now exist. To begin with, we have great hospitals and clearing houses for those who have just passed over, and who, for various reasons, are not received by relatives. When the soul is severed from the body, it is not in its normal condition, either on the sphere it has left, or on the one to which it has travelled. It is astray: The whole being is disorganized.

Care of the Newly Arrived

It needs care, and all souls who come here are cared for, whether they are received by their friends or not. Some who are recovering from the shock of death help those who have just passed over, in fact, this is the first work that souls do in our world, and it has great educational value. In such cases as wars and epidemics, where people pass over in great crowds, all possible helpers are mobilized, and arrivals are treated in what I may call our great hospitals. In the case of war, so many instantaneous deaths occur, the work is very arduous indeed.

In case of accidents in your world, we have helpers ready. Certain persons choose this work, and are always standing by ready to help, much as your fire brigades do. We who went down in the *Titanic* were not alone, we were quite conscious from the first that the unseen helpers were there.

Our hospitals are all conducted on lines of complete rest. We admit no light to them. You are often told, by those who have recently passed on, that they are in the dark. This is literally true.

Some of our medical men devote themselves to the newcomers. This is a work in itself. No one who wished to be really helpful could undertake anything better. Most people have friends or relatives who have watched for their passing, and who bring them to their homes and keep them quiet. But there must be treatment, and our medical men see to that, just as your infant specialists see to the babies.

Ailments

As to our disorders, we have as many or more than you have, but they are all mental. The body we wear when we come to this sphere is proof against injury in the ordinary course of events. It is a serviceable body, and always looks young and vigorous, but we suffer mentally, either from depression – looking back with regret on what is past, is a common ailment – or, we may be obsessed to a certain degree, if we lay ourselves open to it. We may suffer from the mental conditions, that lead to what you call wickedness.

Jealousy may beset us, envy, hatred, anxiety to hurt or injure. These are the ailments that are treated on our side. These sensations take the place of bodily ailments in your world. They can be very painful and distressing, but they cannot kill us or drive us into the sphere beyond the one we are on. They can drive us back into the world we left, and they do this now and then, that might indeed be called death. If, for instance, a desire to injure a living person was strong enough, it might drive the person who suffered from the ailment to reincarnate, or if the desire was less poignant, it would drive the soul down into the astral web, where it would spend its time in a bad dream, trying to get back to the world, and never having the strength to do so.

Questions and Answers

Q. You say there are various reasons why some are not met by relatives and friends?

A. One reason might be that the relatives had passed on to high planes, and could not reach them. This occurs very seldom. No, the waifs and strays we take into our hospitals are as a rule, people who do not desire to get into contact with anyone. They are almost always people who did not believe in survival. Those who are self-centred would not be met. In all these cases the desire, or thought, has not been sent out to us on our side. The desire calls us, you must remember.

Q. You say: "The body we wear when we come to this sphere does not go wrong except in a few cases". Can you explain these cases?

A. We may hurt or injure the body in three different ways. We may go down into the sphere below, and stay too long, then we suffer asphyxiation, or what would be equivalent to it. We might tear ourselves if we stayed too long in the astral plane. When I say that I mean that in the intermediate plane where darkness prevails, we can hurt our bodies. And thirdly, an attempt to reach the plane above us can have disastrous consequences.

Q. You say that when driven back to this world, that might indeed be called death. Might that be the second death referred to in the Bible?

A. It is a very bitter experience indeed. It is referred to in the Bible. It is the only possible second death.

Q. Writing of the soul driven down to the astral plane you say it would spend its time in a bad dream of trying to get back to the world, and never having strength to do so. How does it get release?

A. It may stay there a long time. Only help and prayer can release it.

Q. Do doctors on your side influence medical men here?

A. Yes, and those who influence medical men are doing the best work on your plane in my opinion. I do not want to discourage doctors who, have chosen mediums, and work directly on the patient, but there is no doubt whatever that the patient runs risks with such mediums. The doctor on our side cannot be sure of accurate transmission unless the medium has medical training.

Q. Can they do more through control than by inspiration?

A. In my opinion no. I have no hesitation in saying that the best work is done by unconscious influence.

Q. Doesn't darkness mean a low state of progression?

A. That causes the same sensation, but not quite to the same extent. Dimness would better describe the condition you speak of, which comes from sheer inability to see and enjoy a world which, even in its lower planes, is more brilliant and vivid than the one they have left.

Q. Some who pass on have told us they are taken to rest amongst flowers?

A. Well, some of those who are fortunate may be amongst flowers in some of our sanatoria, or they may imagine or dream they are lying on those flowery beds, but it is the exception, not the rule.

Q. You say you admit no light to your hospitals – why?

A. Because it is the surest and best condition for the first week or so, then gradually the light comes to them. Remember that our light here is brilliant, and would be very distressing to them at first. Dimness is necessary for the first few days. Imagine a newborn infant suddenly exposed to light and air. You treat your infants much as we treat ours, but we can get them to a normal state very quickly.

Q. Is it desirable to try and help these people from our side?

A. On the whole, no, not desirable, but it may be that in so doing a desire is satisfied in a temporary way. There are a few cases in which such work can be really useful, but it is not suitable for amateurs or persons who attempt to do it from mere curiosity, or from a desire to show what excellent people they are.

Q. Is Dr. Wickland's work good?[3]

---

[3] See *Thirty Years Among the Dead*, by Carl A. Wickland.

A. Yes, but it involves a certain amount of danger. It is not likely that harm will come to him or his wife, because they have learned the trick of allowing these influences to pass through without remaining: but there are few people who would dare to do what they are doing.

Q. Is it good to pray for those in the darkness?

A. Well, that would apply more to those who have recently passed and are in our hospitals, or to those who complain of dimness. It would not help to expel obsessing entities.

Q. We have been told that the living here can get in touch more easily, because they are likely to be on the same vibration.

A. That is true up to a point, but always remember that on our side we have workers who can deal with every kind of disorder, and though your thoughts may, and do help, they are only assisting our workers who understand such cases perfectly.

Q. Are absent healing groups for sickness on this side good?

A. Yes, they are really useful. But I would not compare that with the work referred to in your last question. You can do a great deal through absent treatment if those who act as the mediums can visualize the ailment. It depends a good deal on the accuracy of the mental picture. Added to this, the desire to be healed must be intense and concentrated. All this requires training. It can be done, but like everything else, to be really effective, conditions must be perfect. I approve of circles being trained for this work. There are always helpers on this side who collaborate with them, and the more work you can do of that kind the better. Eyes are very sensitive to absent treatment.

10

The Curative Power of Music

~

After you enter into the next sphere you find that music is no longer regarded as an art only. It is considered the greatest of the arts, but it has other duties to perform. After you have left the physical body, the new body that you wear is highly sensitive to sound and colour. Its maladies can be helped best by vibration, but when I say vibration I do not mean, that the troubles of the new body can be cured by a succession of jangling noises. The curative music is of a very high order, and is selected to suit the patient. In your world you realize the soothing power of music, but you cannot see the vibrations of music, you do not understand the high vitality that it can produce in you. But we can see the succession of harmonious vibrations as a column of light, or as a shower of tiny sparks, or as a softly flowing stream. The malady reacts to this treatment according to the music prescribed.

How Music is Used

We have music in our sphere that excels yours in every way, and in all our hospitals there is a great musical installation. When souls pass on from your sphere to ours, we always treat them with music, this harmonizes the confusion which, as a rule, follows the condition called death. Our troubles are mental or temperamental, and these can best be treated by lying or sitting in a darkened room, listening to music which has been selected by our doctors as being most suitable to the individual case. If you understood a little more how to select, and what harmonies to choose in your sphere, you, too, could use it as a healing agency. It is much better and surer, for instance, than the laying on of hands.

We also use music as a means of stimulating work. You employ it for your soldiers when marching, we for inciting activity: in fact it would not be going too far to say that we are never without music. Our vast orchestras are heard all the time. Orchestral music is not the only music that heals. In many cases one instrument or the human voice, can do more than the whole orchestra. It all depends upon the personality of the patient and the nature of his malady.

I want to give my readers some idea of this treatment. Suppose someone is suffering from obsession. In certain cases carefully selected music would drive the obsessing entity away. Strident vibrations, at a rate prescribed by the doctor, would have the power of expelling the intruder. It would have to be continuous treatment, while the patient is awake the music would continue all the time, and when he slept he would carry the vibrations with him.

Of course it is good to have music during a sitting. I should say, perhaps, "desirable" but you cannot be too careful in selecting the music to be used. Often the vibrations raised through hymns sung out of tune actually retard results.

Questions and Answers

Q. Do you use instruments?

A. Yes, but they are not made of the same material as yours, and are infinitely more powerful. Strings are used chiefly in spite of the fact, that in all pictures of the future life, angels are shown blowing trumpets. We do not use any metal.

Wood instruments only, with wind. The vibration which comes from a metal instrument would be positively injurious in our conditions. The material is the equivalent of wood, strings, and reeds. All these have a pure and lovely tone.

Q. Do the great composers who have passed, inspire music here?

A. Yes, many of them do, but composers are less likely to return to your sphere than painters or writers. Their art grows and expands in our atmosphere, and as a rule they dislike the cramp of the Earth's limitations. It is very rare that any artist, musician or otherwise, is directly in touch with one of the great artists on my side. But it can happen. Beethoven may find some musical genius who interests him and, as he would have done with a favourite pupil, he may influence and help this person.[4]

This does not happen often. What does happen is that here we work in groups, harmonious groups, and while still in the body a young artist may join any special group without being conscious of it.

Q. Does a great musician like Kreisler get into touch with a greater proportion of his soul?

A. Yes, of course he does, when he plays in an inspired fashion, for the time being he is actually in a higher sphere.

Q. Can you explain anything about inspirational drawings?

A. Automatic drawing is produced in several different ways. At times it is a reproduction of something seen in a higher sphere the night before, a subconscious memory automatically recorded. Sometimes an artist amuses himself by taking the brain of someone in your sphere, and making him or her draw, whatever he draws himself. The result depends on the mediumship of the person who holds the pencil. Sometimes, especially when elaborate patterns of foliage are, there is someone on our side who does the decoration: this comes through much more easily than figures.

---

[4] See *Psychical Experiences of a Musician*, by Florizel von Reuter.

Q. Is there any other cause?

A. Yes, vague swirls with the pencil are usually the record of a musical vibration from our side heard subconsciously. It is much more common to have this record of musical phrases than actual drawings, which only come if the operator on our side is an artist, or if the person who holds the pencil is artistic.

Q. Can rhythmic sounds awake response of a more ethereal nature in a medium?

A. Yes, that is so. The more power to appreciate rhythm the medium has, the finer will be the vibration.

Q. David's power over Saul, was that through music?

A. There you had a very perfect instance of receiver and transmitter, David's power over Saul would have been nil, but for the harp, he suited his music to the listener quite instinctively.

Q. When Saul threw a javelin at him?

A. That would be accounted for by a break in the connection. Such breaks do occur in psychic relationship and no doubt that was what occurred then.

Q. You say vast orchestras are heard at all times, can you explain exactly how?

A. When I used the word orchestra I misled you no doubt. I should have enlarged, and said that some of our harmonious rhythm is unaccountable to us. It comes to us as rain or wind would come to you. That music is always with us and it is not in the least distressing, but we have our orchestras as well.

11

The Child:

Its conditions in our Sphere

~

The child who passes into our world, and whose mother is not here to meet it, finds itself more or less alone, unless the grandmother will take the mother's place. I want you to realize that the tie between mother and child is mysterious and eternal. Death cannot sever it, even if the mother has passed on long before the child, and if the child has passed on before the mother, it will meet her when she comes.

The children, who come over in thousands every day, have to be cared for, not only by their own people, but by the more experienced members of our own community. We have special workers to take charge of the children who come across, and have no one waiting to receive them, just as we care for the adult waifs and strays from your world. These children are not in the position of adults coming over, they must be watched and tended for a much longer time.

They have to be educated, just as they would have been if they had remained in your world.

Training

We care for our children better than you do for yours, because we know that each child is an individual, and that a training that suits one, will not suit another. So we modify our training according to the individual needs of the child. This may seem almost impossible to you. I wish you could see one of our homes here. The children are in the first place, classified, according to their group individualities, and then each member of the group is studied by our workers. No two are trained in the same way, although we teach them under the same conditions.

No School Hours

The word "school" does not come into our language in connection with children. We provide homes for those who have not been fortunate enough to have their own parents to help them. In our homes the teaching is simple, but progressive, it is slow but sure, and often we use symbols to help them to understand.

Generally, lessons are learnt in the open air, and there are no forms, or copy books to depress them. We teach chiefly through nature, using flowers and insects as illustrations. They are happy, they have no school hours. They learn without the knowledge that they are being taught. You will probably ask, how do they learn history, geography, and all the usual curriculum of school education? Our method is, to create in them, a desire for knowledge, a love of work. When this is established they have ample scope for learning, in our great libraries, picture galleries, and musical colleges.

We have no trouble with our children after the age of about seven years. By that time they have acquired a love of learning, and there is great competition between them, they stimulate each other. Instead of discussing games, they discuss subjects of intellectual interest, but of course we also allow them to play games.

Needs Sensed

Learning is on a higher plane than yours, but we are still far from the condition of intuitive learning, when knowledge will be breathed in as the air. We have higher centres of learning, where those who have had experience, help the younger members of the community. These are in fact universities, but universities where the needs of the individual are respected. This can be arranged because in our state we sense the needs of others, we can tell in a moment what attitude to assume to each other, we have not to work in the dark as you do.

Eventually you will do away with your public schools, which are neither fitted for the needs of the individual, or the needs of the community. You will learn to understand that discipline, which may be excellent for a service, is not suitable for those who are opening out, like flowers to the sun.

Questions and Answers

Q. Do relationships really count when we pass on?

A. Now that is a vital question; the only relationship that means much on our side, is that between parents and children, and that relationship persists much more between mother and child, than between father and child. The child drifts naturally towards the mother. All other relationships depend on affinity of thought. The inhabitants of your plane, are much closer relatives to each other, than aunts and uncles who are elsewhere.

Q. What happens when mother and child are not in harmony? How long do they remain together?

A. I have told you that the child drifts naturally to the mother, which did not imply that the child would remain eternally with the mother. When mothers and children are not in harmony, the drifting means hardly more than meeting and parting. What I meant was, that death brings mother and child together, just as birth does.

Q. If the mother is not there, who meets the child?

A. That depends, a husband, sister, brother or a great friend. The grandparents seldom meet it. They have been occupied with their own children, though in exceptional cases the grandmother might meet a child.

Q. Does the child keep in touch with the mother, if she is on Earth?

A. The mother comes over at night, and looks after her child, the father not so often. You realize that the mother is much the more important of the parents. The father has only a loose relationship with the child, the mother a close and intimate one.

Q. Does the child on your side grow up with a knowledge of the family into which it was born on this?

A. Yes certainly it does. Few children lose sight of their near relatives, hardly any lose sight of their mothers.

Q. Do the mothers lead a domestic life, when they go over in sleep?

A. This varies according to the manner in which the child lives. They cannot be sure of coming every night.

Q. "According to the manner in which the child lives." What do you mean by that?

A. I mean, that if the child is being cared for on our side, the mother would have no domestic duties, beyond attending to the child when with it. It would be cared for by us, while she was awake on your side.

Q. Do the children sleep?

A. Yes, of course the children sleep. That is a foolish question, they must have a rest time, in which to visit the spheres above them.

Q. Do stillborn babies reincarnate?

A. Stillborn babies usually grow up on our side, and return to some member of their family in a future generation, to the same stem, always choosing the mother's side. Stillborn children, and children who have not arrived at the state of birth, generally remain on our side, until they reach maturity, then they reincarnate.

Q. When they reincarnate, have they gained through their experience on your sphere?

A. Yes, they gain, but they could not progress, or pass on to a higher sphere, unless they have had the Earth incarnation. In other words, until they have been on Earth, long enough to reach maturity.

Q. Do infants return quickly?

A. Some do, some do not. But as a rule they return pretty quickly. The next child of the parents will probably be the return of the little one who was lost to them.

Q. Do the children who have been born and lived a little while, return sooner than stillborn children?

A. Yes, they do. Stillborn children have never reached individual consciousness, while the child that has been born has. When it comes over to us, it has in its superconscious mind, the knowledge that it has not had its Earth experience, so that it superconsciously desires to return.

Q. What is the state of the child spirit, who reaches maturity on your side, and then returns?

A. The child on our sphere would continue to progress, from the point it had reached, when it returned to Earth, maturity in its case, means only spiritual maturity. It has to develop its intellect through the physical brain.

Q. Can a child return quickly to different parents?

A. It is possible, but most unusual. If it occurred, it would be a matter of choice on the part of the child. The first mother would probably, have had much in her, that was antipathetic to the child, which the child would be conscious of in its inner mind.

Q. If the child reincarnates then, its original mother won't find it?

A. The children do not reincarnate quickly as a rule, but in such cases as you refer to, the mother would be met by those who would make the position quite clear to her, and, at a later stage, she would form a connection with her child again.

Q. If there were great love between the mother and child, would it reincarnate?

A. The child would not reincarnate in such a case. It would be surrounded by the emotion of the mother, which would help it to develop on our side, and it would wait until she came.

Q. Is it possible for the child to gain the Earth experience, via the parent who is still in the body (a father stated that he has been told, that his child was gaining experience in this way)?

A. No, it is not possible. Unless the father happened to be the affinity of the child. Then it would be possible to a certain extent, but the child would still have to pass through a short Earth experience.

Q. What of the young children who pass over?

A. The children who are taken are either too developed for their bodies (in which case they would not return) or, are incomplete human beings, who will be developed on our sphere, and then go back to yours.

Q. "Too developed," would these be cases of previous incarnation?

A. Almost always. Often these spirits touch the Earth life for a short time to develop some facet of themselves. Amongst these are the infant prodigies, the young people who are almost complete in their mental equipment before their time. Again, the soul of a child who dies young may be too extensive for the body, and so the body would not hold it, it would open the bud too soon, and the flower would never bloom.

Q. What would be the condition of those who passed on during the war?

A. Most of those were what I should call mature. Some of course were not, and those would be likely to return.

Q. Will they return quickly?

A. No they will not come back for a long time. The nature of their death would necessitate a rebuilding on this side before they would be fit to return.

Q. Is there marriage in your sphere?

A. No. No marriage such as there is on Earth. There is no physical side here, but there is the union of affinities, which is a far closer and more permanent relationship.

Q. There are some here who say that they have lovers in your sphere.

A. There are some who do find their affinity, but the physical side of love is non-existent. A spirit who refers to "lovers" in your sense of the word, is a spirit, caught in the web of the astral.

Q. How far through the spheres does colour persist?

A. Colour and race are symbols of the souls within. When the body is cast off, the same characteristics continue until the fourth sphere is reached, then the difference of race disappears.

12

Animal Survival

⁓

Animals survive in all the spheres and progress if they have been humanized on Earth. The mass of animal life, the flocks and herds that are slaughtered for food, return to the "group soul" of animal life after they leave the Earth. The domesticated animal that has been humanized survives, and after death progresses, though it never ceases to be an animal. The wild animals that have led their own lives unmolested by human beings, survive. They may return to the Earth at once, if they retain memory of their state there, and desire to get back, but as a rule they progress in their own world, which is not the vast animal group, they progress on their own lines.

Now you may ask, why do the flocks and herds pass into the "animal soul" though the wild animals do not. Because the flocks and herds have not had an individual existence at any time, or a wild existence. The wild animals have had to take care of themselves as individuals.

Let me assure those who love animals, and who have made friends with them, that these creatures progress and survive, and it is likely that they will be found by their owners when they pass on. The animal would be drawn automatically towards the person it loved.

Questions and Answers

Q. You say the wild animals would progress in their own world, what do you mean by that exactly?

A. The wild animal creates his own world or universe out of itself, just as man creates it.

Q. What condition can reproduce an animal phantom?

A. In all cases of animal phantoms there has been a deep and clinging affection on the animal's part for some special human being. They act more automatically than human beings, and so, often return without any intention on their part. Few animals return, unless to search for their lost gods.

Q. How do you explain the Elberfeld Horses?

A. In such a case the communicator has chosen an animal because of the nature of the communication. Of course the communicator has done this as a joke or a stunt not to be taken seriously. But the explanation is, that the horses are controlled by someone who has mathematical education.

Q. How about child calculators?

A. Now you come to one of the cases where there is more than one explanation. The child may have reincarnated and contains the knowledge within itself. It may be controlled by a mathematician, or it may have an intuitive faculty in which the inner eye would come into play, and it would know without calculating.

13

Eternal Life

~

I have headed this chapter "Eternal Life" and I hope my readers will understand that most of what I say is theoretical, that I cannot be sure that all I say is true, but I think it is most probable.

I do not address any separate body of persons, not the Spiritualists any more than others. I hope that my readers whoever they are will believe that all I say, is said reverently, and without any bias to any special faith. They will say that I am dealing with a subject that is beyond my ken and theirs. I will agree with them in that statement, but I am one step further on than they are, so perhaps I can teach them something new.

God: the Source of Life

I must first speak of God: that is, God in my sense of the word, for in the sphere where I am now, we can still only speculate who and what "He" is. We look on God as Life, the source of life and being, and we know that he is responsible for the universe and all that it contains. But whether he has a form similar to the human form, whether he is a single personality or a vast group of personalities acting together in accord and harmony, we do not know, and we can only get as far as the threshold of His house. We know through our guides and teachers what that threshold is like, but we have no knowledge of the House of God, for those who enter it do not return.

So let us call God, "Life," for all that lives has to come from Him. All that has shape and form must be the work of His Hands. There is no form of life that he has not created. Where God is, we do not know, nor will our scientists ever discover this secret, which will always remain unfathomable. It would be futile to try and plumb the depths of this secret, for we should find ourselves confronted by problems which are entirely beyond human conception.

The Seventh Sphere

The threshold of God's House is what we call the "seventh sphere". There the soul pauses, for a decision has to be made.

It can pass into the source of life if it chooses to do so, or it can pass into any of the seven states of consciousness, and live in that consciousness, if it has work to do. Generally, when the seventh sphere is reached, the soul is wearied, and in this happy weariness it longs to find rest in God. But there are a few, not many, who have become so absorbed and interested in the development of the universe, and in its inhabitants, that they are ready to bear the compression of the full consciousness which is reached in the seventh sphere, in order to return for a special purpose.

Though the consciousness has to be reduced when the soul descends, it carries the knowledge of itself in the compressed consciousness, and it uses this knowledge for the help and teaching of others.

I shall accompany the soul from the moment of its conception and will travel with it to the seventh sphere, and my readers will come with me, and watch what happens, that is as far as my limited understanding can show it to them.

The Earth Sphere: The Kindergarten

The first sphere, which my readers inhabit, the Earth sphere, is the cradle of the soul. A troubled cradle you will say, full of disappointment, struggle and grief. Yet it is the cradle which gives the soul its first experience of the meaning of life. It learns in its cradle the rudiments of what it will use when it is an adult. The training given to the infant in its cradle varies with the conditions into which it is born, with its parents, its surroundings. The infant soul comes into a world where chances are varied, where it may be born to sin and suffering, but it will find its feet in the best way, even if the termination of the Earth life is tragic. For behind all life there is a purpose of development and completion, and no atom of God which enters the universe will go back to Him until it has fulfilled its purpose.

The Earth life trains the soul for the next sphere. It is familiarized with this during sleep, for then it extends its consciousness so far as the sphere beyond it is concerned, and goes about its work preparing the place to which it will come, when it permanently leaves the physical body.

The Earth sphere should be regarded as the nursery. The soul is not older or wiser than a child of one year when it passes beyond the Earth to the sphere where its real education begins. You believe, my dear readers, that you acquire experience in your Earth-lives, that you, most of you, leave the world older and wiser than when you came into it.

When you enter the second sphere you will feel as helpless as an infant. That infantile condition does not last long, especially if you had any knowledge or teaching, about the afterlife. It soon passes, and you begin to be thrilled and interested with your new condition, and you acquire knowledge rapidly.

The Second Sphere: The Schoolroom

The second sphere is the schoolroom, where you begin to learn something of the meaning of development. Here you are not so puzzled about the unevenness of fate, as you were on the Earth. In this sphere where I am now, you begin to learn the value of joy, and you begin to use the power to enjoy. You have to learn how to use it. One of the purposes for which you are created is the elimination of fear. Another is the power to enjoy, and be happy. As you ascend, you discover that the two worst sins you can commit, are sloth and sorrowing. Sloth, I have explained before, is a sin which if indulged in, will hold you firmly down, and even drag you back if you do not conquer it. Sorrowing, that is causing sorrow to the world in general, and to those around you in particular might be described as an evil disease, for sorrow is infectious.

Now you have entered the second sphere, which is much bigger than the one you have left. Here you will have a long life, and you must make the most of it, you have not yet entered college, but the new school is in advance of a preparatory school. You are more eager to learn now, and you enjoy it, for you are learning to use your intuitions. You are reaching the stage, where you will know without learning. You have not yet reached that stage, you will not quite attain to it in this sphere. But you are all the time training your intuitions. This hastens development and advancement. In the next sphere you will know without training. The meaning of life will be clear to you, and you can look down on your memories, and trace your development.

The University

When you leave this great school, and enter the university, by which I mean the third sphere above the Earth, you will not find your tasks at all laborious. You will begin to train, almost exclusively, your power to enjoy. By that time, most fears will have been discarded. You will not be afraid of the next step, because each advance that you have made has been easier than the one which preceded it. You can look down the thread of your memories, and reflect that those Earth experiences were not so unpleasant, as they seemed to be at the time. They were all in sequence, grief and misfortune, in that far-away Earth life, and given for the purpose of casting out fear. In the Earth life, too, you shed fear, but in the shedding you suffered, and sorrow followed you. Now you feel neither, you realize that in spite of what might happen, the next step will set things right. So on this sphere, which I will call the fourth, you have no fears left.

You go on unhampered by these burdens. Further you realize still more fully the power of enjoyment.

After the fourth sphere is passed, your education is complete. You have arrived at a stage where you no longer learn, you create. The last three spheres through which you pass are spheres of creative activity. You are now in the fifth sphere, and the first thing you do, is to acquire as great an understanding of yourself, and your memories as possible. When you know what is in yourself, you will know what power you possess to create. Here, in the fifth sphere, you begin to pass into the Group, to create out of yourself, with the strengthening power of the Group that is behind you. There are no incongruities here. Quite naturally you fall into your Group, or place, and do your work with its support. You decide soon after you enter, what your real work will be, whether it is for the more perfect development of your own soul, or not. You must decide for yourself. Your object now, is to ensure that your own development is as perfect as possible, and to give it growth through the expression of itself. Your activity is doubled again.

You live much more intensely, and out of your life, you give your life to work. The life you live on the fifth sphere is vigorously active, and the power to enjoy is intensified. Fear is forgotten.

The Creative Spheres

When you leave that life, and enter the sixth sphere, it is a tremendous change for the soul. For here, you are no longer active. This sphere is a preparation for the seventh, a pause on the road, when the soul rests in contemplation, and decides its future destiny. It decides here, whether it will return to the spheres below it and continue to work in them, or, whether it will pass into God, when the right time comes.

89

The sixth sphere is the sphere of perfect maturity. Here the soul is free to judge what is best for it. It has practically completed itself. All that remains in the seventh, is the power to examine the complete chain of memories in this sphere there is no grief or pain. All that is evil, is left behind, life here is full of experience in contemplation. It is a long and happy holiday for the soul. At last it is really at rest, that rest, which enables it to come to a decision as to its future, which ripens to determination, without any active effort. Beauty predominates, not only inwardly, but outwardly. It is the sphere of pure enjoyment. It is Heaven indeed, for those who reach it, may be said to have realized what Heaven means. After that sphere is passed – a long life is spent there remember – we are on the threshold of God's house. Now the soul becomes intensely active again. It realizes the great height to which it has risen. It looks down the long chain of memories, and from these, it makes its final decision as to its future. In the sixth sphere, this decision had been made in the subconscious part of the soul that projected to the seventh sphere but it had not been conscious of it until this last step was taken.

It is not easy to describe the position of the soul on the threshold of God's House, but we may indicate the nature of it, if we say the seventh sphere is intensely turbulent and active. Life there is of long duration, and all the time the soul lives in a state of movement which is not unhappy, for in this last sphere rhythm has become round and perfect, and activity does not mean effort: a happy whirlwind, in fact. Those who do not go back into the life which is God, leave the seventh sphere refreshed and eager for new activities. The causes that induce the soul to return and labour on the lower spheres lie within its own nature.

Certain people on Earth are possessed of the missionary spirit, others prefer contemplation, or find God in complete retirement. The guides and controls who return and labour on the lower planes cannot be said to have the compelling quality of the missionary. They are rather born teachers, the sharers of experience, whose highest happiness lies in hastening the power of enjoyment in other souls. In fact, the guides have, perhaps, attained the highest spiritual perfection.

Guides and Controls

In my opinion, they are the rarer and purer spirits. But you must remember that when they return, you on Earth cannot be said to be in touch with more than a very small section of their personalities. They select their interpreters, I mean the instruments through which they express themselves, whether they are artists, doctors or workers in the séance-room, it is all the same.

Complete self-mastery

We have travelled through the seven spheres, and have attained complete mastery and knowledge of ourselves. How do we feel when we look down the long chain of memories? We feel that the links are all perfect, even that first link that was "Earth". Life had a meaning that attuned it with all the other experiences. What amazes us is the symmetry of the whole chain of existence. This is a form of enjoyment we had not understood before. Until we were perfect, and our development was complete, this symmetry was impossible. We are both amazed and delighted.

But, you say: "You applied the word 'Heaven' to life on the sixth sphere. Can anything exceed Heaven?" My reply is: Yes, in the sixth sphere, you were in a Heaven of contemplation.

In the seventh, you are in a Heaven of activity, and here your enjoyment is even greater than it was in the sixth, for here you are active, with no effort or fatigue.

At last you realize the greatness, the mightiness of it all. You have forgotten your struggles, the chrysalis has burst, and the fully developed butterfly has escaped into the sunshine. You live in God now, and in the joy and wonder of His mightiness. At last you will have learnt to pray, and to worship in the full sense of these words.

You have no more to ask. You know, and in your knowledge, lies the ecstasy in which you exist.

Questions and Answers

Q. Where do affinities unite?

A. They unite on the first sphere of creation. They *may* unite before that, but in any case they must unite there. Man and woman are the symbols of affinity. In order to be perfect, the two must fuse perfectly, must become one in every sense.

This development of two halves, which make a whole, began when each of these souls was created. They may not have entered the sphere of the Earth plane at the same time, but they were moulded from the same material, and are part of each other.

Q. But surely we were all moulded, and made out of the same material?

A. You were all moulded and made of the same material, but the moment you were ready for the journey through the spheres, planetary influence took you in hand, and influenced your make up. It is a case of sphere within sphere. The group divides itself from other groups automatically. The individual divides himself from others of his kind, and chooses his friends, and his affinities, not because he likes but because he must. You cannot enter into God, unless your affinity is within you. That must happen after the fourth sphere is passed, it may happen before.

Q. Once having merged with your affinity, do you remain as one, even if you desire to return and work in the sphere below?

A. Yes, you are one. Even if you decide to return to work on lower spheres, one could not work there without the other.

Q. Do you know anything about the Kabbalah?

A. I have a surface knowledge of it, which is not very deep.

Q. How would you explain the " Ultimate Limitless Light " referred to in the Kabbalah?

A. That is the furthest point that we can ever imagine. It is the light that fills the seventh sphere, but we are sure that behind that, there is a further light, a further fire perhaps.

14

Religion and Faith

~

Value of Religious Faith

I have said that in the seventh sphere, the soul has learnt to pray and worship at last, which implies that until the soul attained that great height, it did not pray in the full sense of the word, nor did it worship. I feel that I must go back to the Earth sphere and explain the value of religion and faith. I have not alluded to creeds or dogmas so far.

On Earth, dogma and creed mean much to those who need them. The so-called narrow attitude of conventionally religious people in any church does not mean that they are intolerant, it means that in order to enter fully into their doctrines, they must believe in them to the exclusion of all others.

To most of the inhabitants of the Earth, it is not necessary to belong exclusively, and intensely to any special form of faith. But there are types, for whom this is the only way. Therefore I say that for certain personalities, creed and dogma are necessary. They find in them the first step, to the realization of faith. That realization cannot be perfect, as I have told you, until the highest stage of development is reached, but it must have a beginning, and the warring of churches, is not so evil a thing as it seems.

War *is* an evil thing, but what appears evil in the contest of creeds, is not so in reality, it cements those people whose mental limitations need creeds in their belief. That which you love, you are ready to fight for. I do not mean that the extreme measures, to which churches have had recourse, such as the Inquisition, are justifiable. I mean that if the need for religion is sufficiently strong, it is likely to lead to contest.

I will define the type which needs religious dogma. They are, speaking in a general way, persons who are dependent on others for their mental attitude to the world. They need support, they desire to be led, not to lead. They are not as active mentally, as the people who can do without a creed, and yet, who lead as useful, and as excellent lives, as any who are within a church.

Let us look at the development of a soul as it travels to the realization of faith. If it is entirely self-dependent, it may go on without any special faith, or form of worship. But most people need a religious faith, or form of worship, even if it be one with very wide borders. Religions such as the Christian faith are of invaluable importance to men. The fellowship of others helps him in his realization of faith.

Faith

I must define " Faith " as I see it, for your benefit. By Faith, I mean the condition in which no question is asked about the future. Faith is the assumption, that a beneficent Providence is always there, caring for our needs. The faithful have no fear. To attain perfect faith, we must have vast experience. And on Earth that is a very difficult proposition. Remember when we are at that stage, we are infants, or, like young animals, who are born blind, and have no understanding, of what is around and about them.

If we are offered a proposition which solves some of our difficulties, we hold on to it, as a drowning man clings on to a rope. Many people may fail to catch the rope, but those who get hold of it will not easily let go. Therefore religious doctrine is a great help to many.

How does that doctrine hold, as we pass on through the spheres? In the world where I now am, there are different forms of religion, but there are no small creeds or parties split off from the whole. So far we are better off than you are. There is no religious warfare. We respect each other's faith, and do not oppose it, because we know that all religions are paths that lead us all to the same goal in the end. It does not matter how the goal is reached. All religions continue here, and on the creative spheres above, then we all belong to one mighty religion, which is the attainment of truth.

I should explain that on the first sphere above the Earth, we have all the observances that you have, the services are held on a larger scale and with a wider purpose. They attract many persons who have not come under the guidance of the church in their Earth life. No one should question the use, of religious observance on Earth. It is not necessary to take part in the ritual, or to come under the dogmatic influence of any church, but always remember that one medicine suits you, and another your neighbour. I intend this to be a tribute to the spiritual doctors on your sphere, their work is more important, than the work of the doctors, who deal with the body. Respect them, even if you do not sympathize with them.

I should like to say a word to those who call themselves Spiritualists, and who regard Spiritualism, as a religion and a cause. We are grateful to them, and acknowledge that their work has been useful. It has made an appeal to many, who imagine, that because we are not visible to their finite vision, we are therefore non-existent, but I beg of you, as a body to be careful, to speak of your faith, as a truth and not as a cause, and to tread carefully, before you call on the agnostics to follow you, you must be very sure of every step, and be careful that your statements are sound.

Angels and Archangels

Christ a Manifestation of God

I am now going to speak of angels and archangels, or, in other words, the saints and prophets, who appear on Earth from time to time. I use the word angels and archangels to show that the saints and prophets, are, and always were divine, in a sense that the ordinary man is not. These great spiritual presences pass at once after their transition, to the creative spheres. There is no novitiate for them. They had their novitiate, long before their Earth incarnation. In every sense they are divine. They possess much more of their Creator's force than ordinary mortals. They come forth as Christ came, but they are different from Christ, in that they do not return and enter into God at once after they leave the world. They have a certain development still before them. Christ came forth from God as a manifestation of God. He was a Son of God in deed and in truth. After His manifestation He entered into God and remained as a personality in His teachings only. Christ as a person does not exist in any of the seven spheres, but His image can manifest there as a symbol of the personality that has passed into the Greater Life.

Jesus the Vehicle

Jesus was the vehicle through which Christ worked. Jesus was a man, was not more divine than other men, but He was possessed of the power to give manifestation of the Divine which is not given to the ordinary man. Jesus passed into the creative spheres after He left the world, and now He has passed into the Greater Life.

Saints and Prophets

The saints and prophets of the Earth have not passed into the Greater Life. These personalities exist still, and are the rulers and teachers of all the spheres.

They are the great tribunal to which spirits, such as the higher guides, must refer in cases of difficulty. They are not active in any special sphere, for they permeate all the spheres with their wisdom and beneficence, and it will be so for all time.

The tribunal of the saints and prophets is the highest that is known to those who have not yet entered into God.

The saints and prophets are emanations from God. They are presences who have sought for, and found, a means of expression while on Earth. They are personalities who need a highly gifted sensitive to give them full scope. They seldom find a suitable vehicle for expression, and so can rarely communicate. By saints I mean any personality who has left a great work finished on the Earth sphere, but I do not necessarily mean those who have been canonized by the Church. A saint may be a visionary, a soldier, an artist, any one of these who leaves behind a vast spiritual record, is a saint in my sense of the word.

The prophets are the vehicles who have been inspired through the inward eye, who attain in their Earth life to knowledge without learning. Their identity as prophets cannot be questioned, because they saw, and showed what they saw to others.

Questions and Answers

Q. How would you define Spiritualism?

A. Spiritualism should be a proven belief in intercommunication between the spheres. It should be broad enough to tolerate all variations of this fact. And always remember that every unit is part of the whole.

Q. Where did the saints pass their novitiate?

A. They came forth slowly from God, and in waiting for their manifestation they observed and learned, thus, it was not necessary that they should travel through the spheres.

Q. How does their coming differ from that of the ordinary man?

A. There's a difference between a ball of fire and a spark. Man is a spark that is sent forth from God. The saint is a ball of fire sent forth from God. The saint does not need the gradual opening up of his senses, because he has in him so much of the divine.

Q. Does the saint manifest in the same way that Christ did?

A. Yes, exactly. The saint must manifest through a near relative in the spiritual family.

Q. Is there any foundation for the belief that each of the planets is controlled by an Archangel?

A. It is probably true, but I cannot state that it is true. I should lean to the belief that the Archangels and the planetary influences were dependent on each other.

Q. Does the planetary body itself influence the Angels?

A. No, but it is rather difficult to put what I mean into words. The Archangels and planetary bodies could be in close relationship to each other. The Angelic force, the force that breathes out fire would be the ruling force naturally.

The New Knowledge

~

Let me sum up as well as I can the advantages that the inhabitants of the Earth gain from the knowledge that existence on the lowest of the spheres is only a first and crude attempt at life. Let us suppose that this knowledge of human survival is common property to the whole world, and then let us take a look at the Earth's future, when this truth will be given to every child as a matter of course, when death is no longer a terrible threat: when perhaps, the word "death" is eliminated from the vocabulary of the human race, and "change" is substituted for it.

I have tried to explain conditions you must expect after you leave the physical body, and I am now leaping at once to the period when the entire human race has accepted the fact of survival. What attitude will be taken towards life when doubts are eliminated, and certainty of survival is established? The child will be told from the time it can understand, that at some future age, unknown, but nevertheless predetermined, change takes place, and that it will leave the body, only to live in a more beautiful one.

The chrysalis and the butterfly will be the eternal illustration for the child. The certainty that there is a future life will alter the values of the Earth life in many ways. It will be shown that crime retards development, and taught that development is the aim of existence. Love and hate have no termination in the Earth sphere, they survive the change common to all. It will be taught that love must conquer hate.

The important thing is, that life will have a new meaning for everyone. The fact that there can be no finality to any form of development of human passions on Earth, will alter the attitude of the inhabitants to each other. They will learn anew the law of cause and effect. They will consider, before they commit crime, because the first thing they will be taught is that the childish fault which meets with punishment, is the tiny symbol, of the consequence which crime draws down on the criminal, not only on Earth, but in the next world.

Those who love each other, and are parted by the change, will no longer mourn more than they would, if one of them were obliged to live in a distant country. That will have a deep effect on human emotions, the comfort of this thought, may perhaps, make a stronger appeal than anything else. You can see, that this new understanding will stimulate all forms of science and art. And all religious opinion will take on different and enlarged values.

I want to sum up the different aspects which the human race will assume when this millennium is reached. Later on I will go into details, and give examples of what I mean.

One of the most important changes will be the elimination of war. At present the world still has the passion to destroy, but when it grasps the fact that war does *not* destroy, that the so-called dead, are *not* dead, but only hurried too quickly into another existence, leaving nothing but disaster behind them, and that – most important of all – those in the sphere above, influence the human race, and work for greater harmony, I venture to predict that war will at last be exterminated.

Cultivation of the psychic forces in each one will be part of human education. Communication will become unconstrained, and as natural, as correspondence between friends at a distance. Everyone will use the psychic power inherent in them for purposes of communication. There will be super-mediums, but the status of these will be very different from that of the mediums of the present day. They will be cared for and treasured as the world's most precious possessions.

Psychic power will be honoured more than the power which makes the poet, artist, or musician. We shall understand the true value of that which is, at the present time, regarded by many as charlatanism.

Let us take the businessman, and examine his position. He will no longer be entirely immersed in his occupation, he will see that business will leave him high and dry, if he limits himself to that alone. He will cultivate other sides of his nature. There will be none of those unfortunate beings, whose sole object in existence apparently ceases, when the power to acquire money ceases.

What will your scientists do, when they realize, that they are acquiring power from a higher sphere? And that new ideas are grains of gold, which come slowly and intermittently from above. They will set to work at once to discover some means, by which they can get in touch with us more fully. Instead of being enemies who torture us with doubts of our existence, they will be our best friends.

At first, priests of all religions will be dazzled and confused, unable to grasp the consequences of the new knowledge. Ultimately, they will discover, that all creeds, lead to the same goal. That it does not matter what dogma they teach, if the desire for truth and goodness is there. Religious warfare will cease. Different religious formula, will still be taught, as a means of reaching a deeper truth, common to all, and the great prophets of the Almighty will at last, take their true place in the Universe.

I fear that my readers will sigh and say: "Yes, but this is indeed the millennium which can never arrive." I do not agree, though it seems at present but a very tiny speck on the horizon.

Now what has to be done to arrive at this millennium? We must not look upon our work on the Earth sphere as propaganda. I have already emphasized that point. I have also endeavoured to show, that what should be aimed at, is that knowledge of the future life should take its place in science. It should stand side by side with all the higher forms of scientific research. It should not be "preached" to the people.

Sermons are not very acceptable as a rule. It should be introduced as a form of interesting study, and there should be schools and colleges where it should be taught. The colleges and institutions which exist at present are not, I think, working on the right lines.

The art of mediumship should be part and parcel of the education of the young. The centres you have at present are centres of demonstration, and while demonstration is both necessary and useful, it is, I fear, an encouragement to the lazy. I feel that the seeker for knowledge should experiment for himself, and should learn through his or her work. You do not send your children to school to be read to, you send them to learn to read. The average student of psychic phenomena is in the position of an illiterate.

You cannot look for greater progress until this change comes about. I can only suggest certain ways by which knowledge might be widened; I cannot force any of you to put my suggestions into practice: for instance, classes should be formed in every school and college for the cultivation of mediumship in all its forms. Teachers who have had experience of psychic training would conduct these classes, persons who were not experimenting themselves, but who could speak with authority. Many will be needed for this, it is the chief necessity; I have not forgotten that, and until you can convince people of the importance of the work, you cannot get enough money to do what is so badly needed.

I have tried to give you a picture of a future world that has accepted this new knowledge. No child from the time it can understand will suffer from the depressing thought that there is an end to life, this comes to the young very frequently now. The child will look forward to life after life.

What is at present called death will only mean the beginning of a new life. A sleep from which there is a sure awakening. Those who have criminal leanings will, of their own accord, try to eradicate these tendencies, will look on them as they would a disease that is known to be curable. The desire to commit crime will be attributed to a flaw in the psychic body, which, with the new knowledge, can be treated and alleviated.

Medicine will alter its tactics completely. Doctors will not look at disease as merely a physical matter, they will have learnt that the soul must cure the body, and that their function is to get a message through to the soul and awaken it to the fact that the body is ill or damaged.

Laws will be changed. Solitary confinement, imprisonment or execution will no longer be inflicted on anyone. Criminals will be treated similarly but on more intelligent lines than those who are mentally afflicted are treated now. The murderer will realize that he has not killed his victim, but hurled him prematurely into a future life, and that for this, he himself must suffer now and hereafter.

Artists will take a much greater joy in their work. They will see that there is no limit to what can be done with sound, colour, and words, that as they open out, and develop, their art will open out with them, and that there is no "unattainable" of which they talk at present. It will stimulate both artists and scientists to understand that they are working on the Earth sphere as a preparation for work on higher spheres.

Science will not continually change its aspects and its truths as it has done, and still does. Theories will not be accepted. The scientists in the spheres above will be consulted on all points.

In all branches of philosophy progress will be made through communication. There will be but one school of philosophy which will be the school of truth.

You may argue that this will be an uninteresting state of affairs when there will no longer be any field for research or specialization, as everything will be based on certainty. That is true in one sense, but remember that the barriers between the spheres can never entirely be removed, that it is always through strenuous effort that knowledge is attained. There will be no mourners – that is, there will be no grief without end any longer. It is true that there must be the sorrow of parting, but it will be balanced by the certainty of reunion. The tomb which closes over the beloved will no longer be a symbol of eternal separation. There will be no graveyards, the body will be cremated, where this is possible, otherwise it will be buried in the open field. The symbols of death will pass.

The child who has left its parents in early infancy will be regarded as having passed into another life in order to attain its maturity there.

The parents who brought it into the world will not look upon it as an example of wasted creation.

All these things of which I now speak will mean a new Heaven and a new Earth, and sorrow will have largely vanished from the world. It will be understood that those who pass on to us are gainers, not losers, and their friends, their nearest and dearest who are left behind, will have been mentally and spiritually trained to rejoice, rather than lament their departure.

Old age will not be dreaded, it will be looked on as a natural withering of the Earth body to the advantage of the soul within, for, remember, death is no more than the casting off of a sheath. Again, the chrysalis dies, but out of the sheath, which is a dead thing, springs the butterfly, a hundred times more full of life and a hundred times more beautiful.

Now turn your eyes again to the world of the present, where injustice seems to rule. When the attitude is changed by the certainty of human survival, then injustice, which seems so overwhelming now, will be seen to be a preparation for a better state of things. As the world is now, there seems no theory, save that of reincarnation, which can give the sufferer comfort. But when it is understood that there are many future lives in which reparation is made for sorrow in this Earth of yours, there will be seen to be a scheme in creation at last. In other words, it will change the attitude of human souls to God.

At present many people refuse to believe that effort is of any permanent value. The new knowledge will stimulate every form of effort, from the building of a house to the writing of a vast work on philosophy. It will be seen that to do your job well is a step towards a goal which may be distant but is sure.

It may seem optimistic to speak of this great alteration in the Earth's inhabitants, but I hope you will see from what I have pointed out, that it is very worthwhile to make the best of life, even when circumstances are difficult and depressing.

I send this message to you all, and I send it with all my heart: I hope that this knowledge of the continuation of life may be given to the world before it is many centuries older. Waste no time. Let every moment be spent in working well or resting well, and when you fall on the road, rise and do not regret the fall, for remorse is a waste of energy. Look ahead at the great distant summit, ever and always.

PART 2

THE PROCESS OF COMMUNICATION

Communication between the Spheres

~

1

Evidence of Survival

~

Communication between the world you living beings are in now, and the world beyond you has been questioned as far back as history takes us, and indeed, in many periods it was not considered at all. For the last half century the message sent back by the soul which has passed out of its body, has been questioned and criticized in a manner which would not be accepted as logical argument in any court.

You have no reason to doubt that the dead survive. You have learnt it in your "official" religious training. If you have no religious faith, you have no reason to doubt it either, for you can then turn to the material evidence which we disembodied souls can give you. Sift it, criticize it, weigh it in the balance: and if you are fair-minded you will be obliged to confess you have less reason to doubt our messages than the fact that the world is round.

Your scientists are continually changing their beliefs and their tactics. The truth of today may be discredited tomorrow. The fundamental belief, inherent in man, is belief in the immortality of the soul. Therefore I shall assume that my readers believe the evidence of the reality that exists within their souls, realize the difficulties, and will come with me into the next sphere and try to learn what our difficulties are, our difficulties in convincing the Earth inhabitants that we still exist and still preserve our individuality.

May I remind my readers that the quotation from the Holy Scriptures, "We shall be changed," is a fundamental truth. No two spheres are alike, the soul has to exist under different conditions in each of the steps it takes in its ascent or descent. Therefore, remember that you and I are not living in the same dimension, and that when you travel with me to the next sphere you will not be the same man you were when you took your bus or your tube to your business in the City. But, you are the same in essentials.

What are the Essentials of the Soul?

Now, what do I mean by essentials? Essentials are the emotions that make up an individual. The activities of the soul, its loves, its hates, its pleasures, its pains, these travel with us from one sphere to another.

Close your eyes, and you will see wonderful people and places. Close them when you are half conscious and keep them closed for say one hour. At first your visions will be cloudy and nebulous. But after a time people and places may clear themselves out of the mist. You are back again in a gay scene in Paris still fresh in your memory: or you are climbing a mountain in Switzerland, or you are seated by the fireside on a winter evening, with those you love best beside you.

These things are the true realities within your soul. Memory is an essential of the soul. So much an essential that at some far distant period of our existence we shall amass all our memories and have the story of our life complete.

But not now, my friend, and when you travel from the Earth to the next sphere, the memory of the facts of your Earth life gets tangled, and although they are there, you cannot always sort them out. Imagine in your daily life having a memory of facts that lie far back in your childhood, remote and illusive as the memory of a dream. Again, imagine a living memory of happy or painful emotions, of ties that are all the stronger because a veil separates you from the actual presence of the souls you love. Imagine the intense longing that exists in you, for communication with those who are now to you, as the dead are to the living.

Then if you can imagine once more that someone tells you that there is a way back to the world, that if you can find the road it will lead you back, for a few moments only perhaps, but yet for a few precious moments into your past life, would not you give all that you have to find that road?

The Road Back

Of course, in my case I had heard of the road. I had almost begun to travel it before I died. So no inquiry was needed; I at once set myself to find it again. The outward road is more difficult to trace than the road back to the world. I had not much trouble. I believe my first fully conscious act was to look for it.

2

First Attempts

~

My first attempts to communicate were not very successful, because although I knew pretty well what to do, I did not know how to do it. At first I could only shoot short messages at as many people as I could think of. I felt such a responsibility; I felt that if I, who had been such a prominent member of the few who believed in communication with the dead, did not communicate, I should add to the list of betrayals of trust which weaken our cause on Earth.

In this way I wasted a lot of energy. Yet the net results were that my messages were pretty widely disseminated, so that many people found that they had the same results from me. I was so gay and ardent at this first moment of returning consciousness, and felt so young, that perhaps it accounted for my excess of activity.

Adequate Response was Lacking

One of my memories was that of being plunged in the ocean and gasping for breath, but that was nothing compared with the suffocation which oppressed me when I first tried to communicate.

The want of adequate response was terribly discouraging. I realized what the words "naked soul" meant at last. So you see, even if you do know that the road exists before you die, a severe and thorny path must be trodden in the beginning. After the first effort I came up spluttering. It tried me very much. I felt twenty years older when I tried to get back to my new life.

The Extent of the Soul

I must explain to you that after you die the soul suddenly seems to expand. That is not really so, because the soul, being so much greater than the body, it is not expansion we arrive at, but understanding of the extent of the soul. When we communicate with you, we have in a sense to form a body, a body that will compress the soul again to the dimensions it had before it cast off the body. The whole thing is a strain. When we speak to you we are in an unnatural condition.

Time a Difficulty

I admit that after this first effort I was obliged to rest for a time. I felt as if several years had passed before I spoke again, and then I began to feel that time did not seem to be measured or to move as on Earth. I began to be conscious that past and present were not words which I should use in future. A term would be found that would make these two states seemingly synonymous. I felt I had no idea of what the measurement of time was in a world where such limitations existed as hours, minutes, seconds, days, weeks, years. They all seemed to unite in one moment for me. The sensation is hard to describe.

You ask me, was I conscious of the future. Up to a point yes, but beyond that point, no. I was conscious of the future so far as it extended to the limit of the sphere I was in, that was all. I began to see that my task would be trammelled by this want of movement in time.

I should perhaps forget, and be unable to send messages back that would be convincing to those on Earth. I was troubled with this idea for quite a long period, but that there was a way out I was sure, and at last I found it. I shall not tell you now how this way out was discovered, for I am sure that you are longing to hear exactly how communication is achieved.

How Communication is Achieved

You close your eyes, that is, you shut out the outer world, and live more within yourself, more within your soul. You determine to return, and with a great effort you control your powers of thought, you leave yourself a blank, just as mediums do on Earth, and suddenly, quite suddenly (for you never know how the transit has been made), you are back in the world you left such a short time ago. You are often told that a call will bring us back. That is true, a desire calls us back to you. The transit from our world to yours becomes mechanical. In a moment we can be with you, and even be with many different people, in different places, in the space of a few seconds, but not with two people at the same time. We do not communicate with segments of our personality, as some people appear to believe. Space no longer exists for us. We are independent of it, both in our own sphere, and in this artificial condition. I decided, after the second or third effort, that I should practise this return to the world regularly. Soon the suffocation was less oppressive than it had been. I was beginning to get accustomed to my dive through the ether, into the heavier atmosphere of the Earth. I was almost but not quite beginning to enjoy it.

Broadcasting to Mediums Only

I found less response than I expected. At first I was quite unconscious of the medium for these messages. After I had begun to reflect on the process, this apparent elimination of the medium interested me immensely. On my next excursion I was determined to watch, to analyse, and to discover exactly how the process worked itself out. As is always the case with us over here, I found that some people were immediately sensitive to my presence, but the majority appeared more or less insensitive. I commented on this, and now it dawned on me that I had been broadcasting through the mediums only, that the people who had none of the quality of mediumship gave out no light by which I could see them. No light, I thought, but soon I found that the quality of light given out by those without mediumistic power was vague and dim, whereas the lights of those with power are definite and distinct. This truth flashed on my mind when I was actually caught in the folds of your world, and at last I understood.

The Psychic Light

I can only describe the power of a medium as a bright light, a light which appears to have the quality of a sounding board too, for without it no message can be delivered. This may sound nonsensical, but I am recording impressions, rather than explaining their actual values.

Now I was more at my ease I could watch, and gradually I saw what actually happened. Through the light surrounding the medium, I saw what appeared to be a mirror, reflecting my thoughts. Thoughts did I say? – My messages, for they were no longer conveyed by sound. They were silently conveyed to the mirror which reflected them more or less accurately. I noted at the same place the light would vary. I would visit the same medium two days running. On the first day the light would be brilliant, and the mirror thoroughly cleaned for accurate reflection. On the second day all would be dimmed, and my thoughts would become tangled. Marvels increased.

At first, such was my state of suffocation and confusion, I could see nothing but the light.

The Power to Reflect

As I became more accustomed to it, I saw the person who had called me, and the spiritual presence which guided the mirror in such a manner that it caught the reflection of my thought. "I have it now," I said. "That is the sitter, this the control: I have fathomed the mystery." But not yet my dear readers.

There was another point which puzzled me for quite a long time. Sometimes I would see the light, the mirror would be clear, but I could see no sitter present. There would be no possibility of a reply to the message for the simple reason, that so far as I could see, there would be no one to receive it. I inquired why I should have been summoned under such circumstances. I asked the control, and he replied: " There is no reflecting power there, the sitter cannot reflect the message."

This reply was not enlightening. I saw one clear mirror before me, where was the other and what should it reflect?

It took some time to understand the part the sitter played at these meetings. I observed what I could. Still the light and the mirror were visible; I could even understand that the sitter was present, but I did not see a second reflector from his mind. I watched, and at last the solution dawned on me. The sitter emitted the force simultaneously with the medium. That follows as a matter of course, for the soul of every living human being shines through the body, and is visible to the disembodied. But now, I saw that one mirror had to serve the three who were present. It had to serve the medium who had created it, the communicator, and the sitter, each used different facets of it. If the sitter was not possessed of reflecting power, no matter what his lights, the message could not transmit, for the communicator and the sitter are at different angles of the mirror. By its aid only can the message become reciprocal. I see you close your eyes and think. So did I. Although I now saw the difficulty, I could not explain it. The control was not communicative, so I left that sitting. He offered no explanation.

Attitude of Controls

Here I must interpolate, that controls vary a great deal. Some are ready and glad to act as teachers to souls on both sides of the veil, but others seem to obey their instincts, and go through their work mechanically. When they return to the world to accomplish their very arduous tasks (for they have become so accustomed to the Earth conditions that they can stay down there for a very long period) they take on their old Earth conditions. The conditions and forms, I should say, for they look more like human beings than we who have passed on to the world of spirit.

For having been steeped in the Earth atmosphere for long periods, they are more completely material than the disembodied who, although they retain the shape and form they had on Earth, appear in a luminous haze. This is due to the fact that the soul is no longer sheathed by the body. Controls vary in their moods and temperaments. They may tell the story of their lives, but if they do, it is impossible to tell which life they are speaking of, for they have passed through seven of these worlds, and now find it difficult when they are in the Earth condition to select the actual tale of their previous existence. This is a parenthesis, for I hope to write a whole chapter on the subject of controls, and why they are given this special mission.

The Reflecting Mirror

Now I must continue to tell you how I solved the problems that confronted me in the start of my career here. I thought and thought over the sitter's part in a séance. At last I satisfied myself, that the soul when in communication, must be a reflecting mirror, and if the sitter's soul is undeveloped, or clouded in any way, it cannot play its part as reflector, and join the medium and communicator, in the effort to obtain a clear message, and then the whole experiment is a failure.

This was my first, and rather crude conclusion. Later on I discovered many subtleties that lay below the surface. These are only the broad lines necessary to successful communication.

Questions and Answers

Q. Then would you say that the medium, communicator and sitter, are of equal importance?

A. Yes, I may say so, though the medium is in a sense the most important, because the medium can destroy the work of the other two if passivity is disturbed for a moment, but practically they are of the same value.

Q. Can a sitter improve his power as a sitter, and can he understand the part he plays?

A. A sitter can improve, provided there is sufficient receptivity and will to receive the message. But a sitter who has bad reflecting power, will never be a good receiver.

Q. What causes the lack of reflecting power?

A. The cause is usually found in the sitter's inability to be passive. But this is not always the reason. There are certain persons who automatically close the psychic centres against communication.

Q. Can a spirit on a higher sphere only be seen by those who have a special power?

A. A spirit on a higher sphere can only be seen by those who have a special power, but it is also true, that at times a mass of people can see. When this happens, there is a special quality, in someone present, whose seeing power is equal to those of all the others collectively.

Q. If a person has no reflecting power here, does he acquire it later?

A. Oh yes, if it is very poor, or absent on Earth, it may be very acute on the next sphere. This is not always the case, but at some period it will be acquired.

Q. Does a good medium here continue to be a good medium through the spheres?

A. Yes, as a rule, but it may be that mediumship will not be used for purposes of communication. It may be used for music, art or literature.

Q. If one realizes he has mediumistic powers, and refuses to develop them, will he suffer for it?

A. All psychic force will react on the person who possesses it, if it is not used. If you do not use your limbs, they become helpless. If you do not use your psychic force, it will make you ill, mentally and physically.

3

Communication with Sphere above my own

~

The Right Conditions

On the third sphere, where I now am, it is possible to communicate with the fourth, as well as with the Earth. These communications are also conducted through a medium, and are wholly and entirely unsatisfactory, unless the conditions are even and well balanced. It is always a case of conditions. Communicating between any two spheres depends on having the right tools, in good condition, and ready for their work. I gave a great deal of time to this question, and soon after my first plunge, I attended lectures on the subject, and understood that my own conclusions were on the right lines, though not accurate.

The second experiment followed quite naturally on from the first. I tried to get a message from the fourth sphere. The question arises in your mind, is there then a second death? Do we die seven times during our journey through the spheres? Yes, certainly we do, but death (oh that inadequate word!) becomes less and less painful and mysterious, as we go further on. This experiment was an effort to get in touch with one who had "passed on", this is your own phrase, so I send it back to you.

In the third sphere, there are comparatively few people, who know that communication is possible with the fourth sphere. We are practically in the same state that you are in your world, but there are doubts and discussions here as to whether it is possible to reach those who have passed on. This may seem strange. Surely we who are in a more spiritual state than you know more, and should be able to communicate instinctively with those who have left us. That is not so: we are obliged to find a medium to help us unless we are mediums ourselves. The question of what a medium is, what the word medium means, is summed up in the phrase "a spiritual reflector". If the medium has been able to reflect that which comes from the Earth, he can also reflect messages from the fourth sphere. The veil between it and the third is thinner than the veil between the Earth and the third. Again, I give you back your own word "veil". What it really needs to describe the barrier is not the word "veil" but "cloud", "atmosphere", "weight". Your Earth is like the sediment at the bottom of a vessel, the higher you go, the clearer the fluid becomes.

I am able to see my Communicator

I had used your medium, a medium in your own world for my first, now I needed a medium in my own condition for the second. I found one easily, though there are not very many here. Those we have we treasure for two reasons, for what they can bring, and for what they promise us. We treat them with the utmost respect. My medium had no difficulty whatever, in putting me in touch with the person I wanted. I was soon in communication with the fourth sphere.

I was so astonished that I was hardly able to analyse the experience, for in this case communication did not consist merely in messages. I was able to see the person I spoke to. It all seemed like a wonderful happy dream. I was conscious of a curious condition, too. Was I dreaming? I seemed in another world, a rarefied world, different from the one I existed in now.

The message I received after the identification of my communicator, and indeed identification was hardly necessary, for I saw her distinctly, was deeply interesting, for although she was in a much more advanced condition than I was, my communicator was able to describe her world to me in terms which I could understand.

4

My First Clumsy Efforts

~

I Overshoot the Mark

After this I fell from the pinnacle I believed I had reached. I had overshot my mark, I had begun too soon, and done too much. I was ill for what seemed to me a long time. Like youth, I was too impetuous. I had rushed into the investigations I so longed to make, without considering that I was beginning a new life, and quite unaccustomed to my new surroundings.

I was Ill

This illness did not quench my ardour in the least. I submitted for a time, and felt all the stronger after I had recovered. I was panting to be on the trail again, and very impatient because I had been held back from sending the world the evidence it expected from me.

So now I determined to go back to Earth again. I was eager to learn from the controls how it was they were able to sustain their dive for such a long period. Remember they were unseen, so I had to communicate with them through a medium, when of course they became visible. This was a fruitless inquiry. They refused absolutely to allow me to make the experiment which consists of moulding a body or cloak out of the Earth atmosphere. I retired hurt. I had gained nothing from them.

I dart from Sitting to Sitting

So now all I could do was to plunge in and stay as long as I could endure it. I amused myself trying to include a number of different kinds of sittings at each of my visits. Sometimes my dive would bring me nothing. I would strike a barren day when no mediums were available. But there were good days too, when I darted from one sitting to another – I may say that I was always welcomed and well received.

Memory of my Earth Life

Perhaps you say: "But were you not interested in your life, and the sphere in which you found yourself?" Yes, assuredly, I was. But I looked on these visits to the world as my daily tasks, my work, for I had no intention of taking on any other, and naturally I performed these tasks every day. My memory of Earth life seemed perfect. It was, and is perfect, in fact, more perfect than it was when I was alive in the world. My memories seemed laid on the table sorted and arranged for me. I had no trouble in selecting anything I wanted to remember. But when I was in the sediment at the bottom of the jug, all was different. My eyes were covered by the slime; I could not see this and that bit of my life isolated from the rest.

The Difficulty of Collecting Facts

You should never be impatient with us. If you are at all fair-minded you will try to understand what we have to contend with. Our task is a very difficult one.

We try to pick out the bits you inquire about from our past. If our eyes are clogged it isn't easy. We remember emotions, our loves, our hates, and our ties on Earth, because they are part of us, they have sunk into our souls. If they are to be collected the control must help us. His eyes are not clogged with the sediment. He can pick a fact out of the mass and place it in our hands.

You must remember that while we are inexperienced we imagine we are breathless, actually this is a nervous strain which soon passes.

5

Trance

~

As I have said I spent most of my time jumping from sitting to sitting. I soon learned that this was foolish, for I never seemed to grasp any detail in this way. I therefore made up my mind to attend the sittings of one medium only, and for some time I was with her every day. Soon her control and I became acquainted. He helped me most generously, and I watched what happened carefully.

The medium sat in trance, a type of sitting in which the control is constantly kept busy. I must endeavour to explain what happens. The medium goes into trance, that is to say his condition is one of complete passivity. The control watches his opportunity, and when he is ready, holds up the mirror to the sitter.

Now the communicator having arrived is admitted, and he too reflects his thoughts in the mirror. He cannot speak himself unless he can enter into the vacancy left by the medium in her brain centres. The control can do this easily, the communicator only with danger to himself. That is why in trance-mediumship the message is more often given by the control.

The process is as follows. The medium becomes drowsy, and his brain activities are at rest, he slowly draws himself out of his brain centres, and the control leaps in without an instant's pause, and holds up the mirror from within the medium's brain. When I say the medium becomes "drowsy" I do not mean that sleep overcomes him. He calls sleep to him, and gradually his wish is obeyed and a kind of sleep comes upon him. In ordinary sleep the soul is withdrawn from the body by a natural process, in trance mediumship it is different, sleep is summoned and the brain centres are entirely vacated. It means that so long as the control desires the use of these centres the soul must remain outside them. The control can regulate the length of a sitting. He knows that at a certain period the soul longs to enter the brain centres again, that it is wearied by the length of the communication, and so he ends the sitting. As the medium develops these periods become longer, in the early stages they are very short.

It may be asked why trance sittings are scarcely ever of the nature of conversations, why it is so difficult for the soul of the communicator to enter the brain centres of the medium, when the guide can do so with apparent ease.

When I say that the guide enters and uses the brain centres I speak the truth, or rather half the truth. The guide or control bathes the whole of the medium in his personality. It is not the brain centres alone but the whole being including the soul which is externalized. This is a safe position for the medium. But if the communicator tried to enter it would be an entirely different matter, it might amount to a case of obsession.

It is possible to convey what may be called a conversation through the guide or control, but it is not satisfactory, chiefly because the communicator is not actively in touch with the emotions of the sitter, which are living things, remember. It is easier to give isolated facts. In cases when the medium is fully developed, and the communicator can enter the brain centres, the nature of the messages changes. Then it becomes a matter of conversation, as in voice or automatic writing.

The message at a trance sitting is often more detailed than at other sittings, for the simple reason that the control not being blinded by the sediment, can pick up any detail he chooses, reflecting it in the mirror for the sitter. The failure or success of such a sitting depends more on the control than on the communicator. It also depends on the power the medium has to leave the brain centres vacant. Some mediums cannot draw themselves out of their bodies completely, and if they fail to do so, the control cannot function properly, so confusion occurs.

Through the Brain, Soul and Body Contact

I have tried to make this as clear as possible, but I have no doubt that my readers will find it hard to understand, how the vacating of the brain centres, and the drawing away of the medium's soul from the body, are one and the same thing. The soul functions, so to speak, through the brain. It is there that the contact between the soul and body really occurs. In trance the soul loses contact with the brain, leaving the centres vacant, and another entity can make use of them temporarily.

This, however, is not the case in other forms of mediumship.

Conditions vary greatly, and in some cases the control leaves the entire manipulation of the brain to the communicator.

Questions and Answers

Q. You often seem to prefer to give the message through the guide even when using a fully developed medium?

A. I prefer it because it saves time. I am an excellent communicator through long practice, and I can make the guides understand the nature of what I want to say even if it involves more than mere facts. I prefer it, but I could take control if I wanted to. If I did so it would be some time before I could manipulate the brain centres and become fluent.

Q. Why should the control or communicator so often speak like the medium?

A. Not necessary. It all depends on the amount of detachment there is on the medium's part.

6

Direct Voice[5]

~

I now pass on to a branch of mediumship which is half mental, half physical, and which I regard with the utmost importance. In voice mediumship, the control functions apart from the medium. He has to teach the communicators what to do, if they have not attended one of these sittings before. The first time I was present at one I made a blundering effort to speak, with the result that I could not make it plain who I was, and the message was choked off in a few minutes.

The Use of the Trumpet

When the medium sits for direct voice, there has always been a preparation beforehand. The control has been busy during the hours that precede the sitting, loosening the material which he must use for the sounds he wants to produce. The medium when the light is put out in the séance room puts the loosened material at the disposal of the control.

The control forces it from him as an egg might be blown, he spurts it out, and is immediately busy forming it into round coils that lie at

---

[5] Mrs. Etta Wriedt. See *The Voices*, by William Usborne Moore.

the medium's, or the sitter's feet. If he cannot get enough from the medium, he may take more from the sitters who are present. But if this is done, the person from whom it is taken, the material, not having been loosened before, is greatly exhausted by the process.

When all the coils of living ectoplasm are lying on the floor at the medium's feet, and at the feet of the sitters, the control takes the mirror, holding it up in turn to each as his communicator appears. The coils are in reality the instruments through which the voices must be formed. The control holds up the mirror as I have said, and then he bids the communicator take up the coil, and press his message into it.

Each coil is connected with the medium by a thin string of ectoplasm, thus the sounds, although not made by the medium, are entirely dependent on the medium.   The use of the trumpet is merely to confine the material to put it into the right shape. The ectoplasmic trumpet is invariably inside the metal mould. Look on it as a pastry mould, it is similar.

It is extremely difficult to use the coils at first, and so before a voice sitting for beginners, the controls have, what might be called a rehearsal and prepare the messages, thus in most cases the messages are short (and rather of the stereotype order) but in certain cases, where there has been long practice, messages can be given and conversations carried on for as long as twenty minutes to half an hour.

The Means Used

At a direct voice sitting the communicators are given an artificially made throat to speak through which they can carry about the room with them, and two or three messages can be heard at the same time while the medium is speaking. The medium suffers a good deal in this form of communication. It is not at all exhausting at the time of sitting, and usually direct voice sittings are long, but there is great nervous prostration afterwards.

Now you may ask, why is a semi-physical instrument necessary for the production of voices which are objective to the medium.

Why cannot the medium's larynx be utilized? There is a form of voice control in which the medium's throat is used as the instrument, and this is a very convincing method of conveying messages, but unfortunately there can only be one communicator at a time, not several, as is the case at a direct voice sitting. The medium cannot speak during a communication if the larynx is used.

Light a Deterrent and Dangerous

Sittings for the voice are much more difficult for the communicator than trance sittings. He has to use his instrument. He may be able to play a few notes, and then the music dies away because he is unskilled. Attempts to produce the voice in a lighted room will never be very successful.

Light presses the ectoplasm back into the medium's body. It recoils when the room is lighted up, chiefly because, being extremely sensitive, it cannot bear the vibration of strong rays on it. It can only be used efficiently in a room where the light is entirely absent. Light is dangerous for the medium, because if the ectoplasm rushes in, and has suffered shock, the medium may suffer badly in the process. Look on it as a form of birth. The mediums who sit for this give out part of their life force each time.

I have explained as well as I can how voice mediumship appears from my side. It seems a much more material process than trance, and for that reason it is more difficult for spiritual beings to succeed with it.

Development for Voice

I should like to add a word with reference to the development of voice phenomena. It is useless to sit for the direct voice unless the circle contains one at least who can externalize the ectoplasm necessary for the coils. How can this be ascertained? It can be tested in the following way. Take the members of the circle one by one into a semi-darkened room and watch the fingertips. If thin threads of light are seen shooting from them, there is at least a hope that this person can develop voice mediumship. If the power is strong these threads will grow thicker and thicker, and you will have found a genuine medium for "voice."

Now let us assume the medium has been found, how shall the circle start? You must be sure there are no insulators among the members of the circle. The numbers of the sitters should be uneven. The medium sitting in the centre, the sitters at both sides of him or her. The sitters should not hold hands or touch each other.

By holding hands they actually retard results, because the physical contact obstructs the flow of ectoplasm if it comes from the sitters.

The quality of ectoplasm varies with different people, in some it has great resonance, in others it has none, results are negative if it is mixed.

Period of Development

If the medium is strong it should take about six months to a year to develop the voice, but where the power is weak, it will be well to test the possibilities of the circle for two years.

If after that time there is no result it is not worthwhile to persist. My advice to voice circles is to try patiently for two years. If nothing happens then there is still a possibility that in five years you might hear a whisper. Ask yourself whether this is worthwhile.

Questions and Answers

Q. Regarding the direct voice in the light. E. W. S. queried the impossibility of getting good results in light and cited séances in America where they say they have had wonderful results in good light.

A. You hear this from a distance. If you saw these attempts yourself you would realize how abortive they are, further, they are very dangerous for the medium. If the control holds out the ectoplasm, forcing it unnaturally to endure the rays of light, it is likely to refuse to be exteriorized next time. I assure you that if the sittings are continued in the light, the medium eventually loses power completely.

Q. Is the exuding of the ectoplasm a subconscious action with the medium?

A. Yes, subconscious if you like, but the medium comes to the sittings knowing it is expected.

Q. How can you tell when a sitter is a non-conductor?

A. It is best to test sitters with the table. If they get movement, or an attempt to give messages, they will be suitable.

Q. Do controls as a rule prepare for all sittings?

A. Not in the same sense as for voice sittings. The control if he has time, finds the communicator the day before by visiting the sitter, and through his or her vibrations finds the people who want to speak.

Q. Does music help – records?

A. Not at all necessary, but it has the advantage of distracting thoughts, and producing passivity, otherwise sitters get restless and interfere with the atmosphere.

Q. Question by E.W.S. with reference to a direct voice sitting in the early days when W.T.S. spoke to her giving directions about his book, and at the close of the séance said most emphatically: "Don't you understand Estelle?" The directions proved to be wrong, and the explanation given later by W.T.S. was, that the thoughts of the sitters wishing things done in a certain way were so strong that the message came through differently to given. Did he still adhere to that explanation?

A. I can explain it, but not as I explained it to you at that time. That was early in my experiences. The reason the message took the wrong turn was that the guide was impatient. I was pushed out and the message was finished by him. At the time I did not understand, thus I imagined it was due to the collective influence of the sitters.

7

Materialization

~

Materialization is rare, because few mediums have a sufficient mass of material, and few are strong enough to bear the controls blowing it out. I have seen only two or three, and in each of these instances the mass that was emitted from the medium was overwhelming. It was twice the size of the body. At first vaporous and cloudy, after a time it consolidated itself and was fit for use. In such case the communicator must be present, but portraits produced through ectoplasm are the work of the controls. When only hands or limbs are produced, it means there has been insufficient material. The communicator has very little work to do as a rule, but there are very rare cases, where he actually puts on the ectoplasm and, at the same time, forms a trumpet and can speak. This requires complete trance on the medium's part, and a gigantic mass of ectoplasm. It is very, very rare and extremely dangerous for the living instrument.

How Ectoplasm escapes from the Body

Ectoplasm comes through various parts of the body where the control finds a weak spot. The mouth is naturally an opening, but in other cases it means, that where the ectoplasm appears there is some weakness in the tissues, or some slight defect.

I should like my readers to comprehend a little of what we understand about the production of what are known as material phenomena on your side.

Let us attend a sitting where materialized forms appear. The medium has to be prepared on our side for a séance. We have to make it possible that an even flow of ectoplasm can come when the trance condition is established. The guides of the medium make the necessary preparations which consist in opening up the psychic centres through which the ectoplasm comes. It may be that this ectoplasm will come through one of these centres only, or as in the case of full materialization, all the psychic centres are loosened to allow sufficient material to develop a complete form.

Incomplete Materialization: Why?

I wish you to understand why so many materializations are incomplete. Incomplete materializations occur when the ectoplasm is coming from one opening only, there is not sufficient material, therefore, to build up more than a hand, a head, or possibly a form not larger than a dwarf. Many mediums can only get as far as this. But when all the centres are open and there is a generous flow of ectoplasm, forms can build up quickly and appear as perfect human beings. You may ask where does the life force come from which gives these forms a fleeting existence, which makes it possible to feel the flow of warm blood throughout the body, and which makes it even possible to hold conversation with the appearances. The reply is simply that the ectoplasm draws with it all this life from the medium. While forms such as these are visible to you, the medium is in the condition of a dead person, for then the cord is exhausted.

The medium gives out this life force, or it is given out by his guides. The communicator is present and immediately seizes the opportunity. He folds himself into the ectoplasm as you would put on a garment.

Suggested Methods of Investigation

Now let us consider the best method of investigating this phenomena which is put forward by scientists on our side to assist science on yours. It is necessary, of course, that you should test it, but your methods are not ideal. For instance, the tying of a medium, if at all satisfactory, means that the body is restricted, therefore it is much more difficult to breathe through the psychic centres, and a much greater effort must be made to drive the ectoplasm out.

No doubt you will reply that no progress could be made if this were not done. I do not agree, I believe that with the aid of a low-grade lamp you would be able to watch the medium and prevent any attempt at fraud, and I recommend that as the trance grows deeper the red light be increased in brilliancy. This would not wake the medium, red rays will never rouse a sleeper. It is white light that produces the waking state. I repeat: give up your efforts to produce voice, or materialization in the light; it can never be more than a poor and incomplete manifestation, but this does not mean that when you have the medium in the deepest stage of trance you cannot submit him to a red light. You cannot produce voice mediumship satisfactorily in red light, and should not attempt it unless the medium is in deep trance.

The best voices will always be heard in complete darkness, though it is possible for whispers or sporadic messages to be spoken in daylight.

Ectoplasm

You now ask what is ectoplasm? You have invented the name yourselves, my dear readers. I do not quarrel with it, but it does not explain itself, you will admit. Well then, in the tissues of the body there is a fluid gelatinous substance which science has not discovered, because it resides in the tissues, being part of their substance. It is the link between the body and the mental structure, and is extremely sensitive to the action of the nerve centres. When this material is loose, that is when it can dissolve itself from the tissues, it is usable. The nerve centres act on it at the desire of the medium to emit it. It is a substance especially suited for the work of a sculptor, and can be moulded very easily. Of course, in the case of moving and speaking forms, there are other agencies at work. The communicator in such cases must put on the ectoplasm and use one of the speaking instruments which are formed by the control. This seems a very complicated process, but where the control is skilful and has a good knowledge of his craft, all becomes easy. The communicator obeys mechanically, and does what the control suggests quickly and without questioning.

Sometimes the communicator appears to dwindle and become dwarfed before he leaves the sitting – this is because the ectoplasm is being drawn slowly back into the medium's body.

I have tried to show you how ectoplasm is used at your sittings. Look on it as a thing alive and apart from the body. It is a living substance, that is why it is so absolutely suited to its purpose.

The Reflectograph and Communigraph

There is one little known form of mediumship which combines mental mediumship with what is purely physical. I speak of the instrument called the Reflectograph, with which I hope my readers are familiar. For this the medium needs a double power, she must give out material of a density which permits her guide to mould a hand, and she must receive the message through her brain after the hand is formed.

Therefore results must be limited, for the medium cannot fulfil both functions, material and mental, and produce more than a small portion of the body and a short message, but it is worth doing, for at times a short message contains good evidence. The control (Ethel) works through her medium's brain. The words that come are given by Ethel, not by the communicators.

The Communigraph will go much further than the Reflectograph. It is a better instrument and longer messages can be given through it when the circle is fully developed.

Questions and Answers

Q. Ectoplasm? Is it an absolutely natural substance?

A. No, as I told you it is the link between the mental and the physical. It is material, in the sense that it is a breakdown in the tissues of the body, and mental in that it is almost completely guided by the nerves which are governed by the brain.

Q. Do the tissues become weaker or do they get stronger?

A. The tissues are liable to weaken if the experiment is frequently repeated, in fact physical mediumship cannot be considered a healthy exercise.

Q. E.W.S. Do you remember materializing at Johnson's in Toledo when I was in the United States, in 1913? They had a red light there. Eleven forms materialized.

A. Yes, I do. It was a colossal business. He had an excellent control, but it is far easier to make eleven different forms, than to create one form which can repeat itself, and move and speak as Katie King[6] did, varied forms which are incomplete do not use nearly so much of the medium's life force as one complete form.

Q. In materializing séances, is it possible for obsessing spirits to get such a hold on the medium that he is not aware of impersonating materializations?

A. The medium who sits for materialization has the ectoplasm drawn out of his body to such an extent that he is physically and mentally sick. When he is in that weakened state, under these special circumstances, it is very easy for obsessing entities from the astral plane to influence him.

---

[6] See William Crookes *Researches in Spiritualism*. T. W. Pub. Co.

Of course, there are cases where the mediums are definitely fraudulent because money has tempted them, but the larger number of cases are obsessing entities from the astral.

8

Automatic Writing

~

My next experience was writing.[7] I had known a good deal about the subject in my lifetime, but I was now to find that my conjectures were all on the wrong line. I sought out a medium for automatic writing, confident that having exploited the much more difficult forms (trance and voice mediumship) I should find automatism child's play. I was to find out my mistake.

On Earth when I studied this subject, I had the impression that the spirit worked through the hand of the writer controlling it physically. I arrived, seized the hand of the automatist. My hand closed on nothing. No impression was made. No communication, not even my name came through. I was rather nonplussed, and then I saw that I had rushed at my task without examining it, that the control who was present was laughing at me.

Soul only Partially Withdrawn

I was astonished to observe what happened. The brain centres of the medium were not vacated as they are in trance mediumship.

---

[7] With Madame Hyver – (see *Communication with the Next World*) Stead Lib.

The soul was only partly withdrawn. Again, although the control operated for a moment or two at the beginning, he did not continue to do so, but withdrew, and left the operation entirely in the hands of the communicator.

Control's Task Difficult and Subtle

I cannot tell you how difficult this is at first, spluttering as one is, in the sediment at the bottom of the jug, and trying to operate a brain only partly vacated, it is a most subtle business, and one which requires practice. The control of a writing medium is in a sense, less busy than the control of a trance medium, but his task is more subtle and difficult. Whereas in the case of a trance sitting, the control does all the work and need not trouble to keep out the invasion of people who are not wanted. In writing, the control must first fetch the communicator, in an instant show him how to operate, and at the same time, he must keep the door closed, which is no easy matter.

You will gather from this, that the function of control varies for different forms of mediumship. None has so arduous a task, as the control of a writer who works through his subconsciousness, therefore a writing control requires great experience and intelligence to carry out his work. He is a more learned and experienced spirit, than those who guide voice and trance. He is more remote from the world, and less occupied with holding up facts to the mirror, for the simple reason that the communicator finds it too difficult to catch at small details, when the soul is only partially withdrawn.

Difficulty in giving Small Details

A writing control cannot occupy himself with the sorting out of small facts, he has to give the actual personality the chance to assert itself. Voice is, perhaps better still for this, but its uncertainty trammels it. A good automatic writer can be as serviceable as a good typewriter. It is the best method for us when we get accustomed to it.

My investigation of writing interested me enormously. As it had been my own form of mediumship, I was vastly entertained at being able to do it from the other side. I continued to write. I first wrote small messages, and then longer ones, but I was always hampered by the fact that I was never sure how the telegraphic impressions I made on the brain were recorded. That is always the difficulty with us; we cannot tell whether the instrument has recorded the message correctly.

Dangers to be Overcome

In the early stages of automatic writing when the control is not completely in charge, the medium is assailed by three dangers unless there is quite abnormal power. The first danger is from his own subconscious mind which is sure to get into the message if the message is slow. The second is from his conscious mind which is constantly hindering the communicator and the subconscious mind with doubts and questions. The third is from the invasions which almost invariably occur from the astral, or "Shadow Plane".

Those who sincerely wish to reach their communicators by this form of mediumship must face these difficulties and work through them if they wish to be on firm ground.

Normal Conditions Best

The best writing has been obtained when normal conditions were observed, the eyes open and the medium attentive to the task, ready to respond to the inspiration, or rather, to the telegraphic message given. When I say the best results, I mean the most evidential and clear results. For although in this way there may be confusions and repetitions, the communications will be fuller and more satisfactory than those obtained in any other form of mediumship. The tricks which can occur under blindfold conditions do not often occur when normal conditions prevail. For blind automatism the board is the better method. The pencil is too familiar and the medium will be conscious, to a certain degree of what is written, but not of what is spelt out on the board.

The soul withdraws itself to a much greater extent when the eyes are closed. The condition is similar to that of trance mediumship, and the phenomena of trance writing is entirely different, for then the communicator operates through an unconscious, not a conscious condition.

Questions and Answers

E.W.S. Q. You say you had the impression that the control seized the hand, but I know you realized when here that it was not just a question of guiding the hand, that it was to a very great extent inspirational.

W.T.S. A. Yes but that was another matter. I fully recognized the fact that there were different forms of writing, but in what I say here I do not contradict myself, do I? I believed it was muscle control.

Q. When does the point of contact in writing take place?

A. From our side, when the communicator begins to reflect, from your side, not until the pencil touches the paper, when the communication flows down through the pencil itself.

9

Clairvoyance and Clairaudience

~

I shall apply the word "clairvoyance", to the production of evidence connected with the sitter, or produced in public, which is not in the mind of the medium, and which is almost always personal. I shall not apply it to the prediction of future events, or in other words, prevision. Prevision, is entirely the work of the control. The medium is a mere receiving station for the message. He takes no part in it, neither does the sitter, neither is there any reflecting process. In cases where the future is accurately predicted, the control may have to look a long way ahead, and from the future draw facts to himself, connected with the information required.

Now when I airily speak of looking into the future, what do I mean? The guide or control knows no time as we know it, he can see much further than we can.

He is in the position of a person on a summit of a high mountain who sees the far distance better than he who is on level ground. The control looks ahead, and it depends on his sight whether the message is truth or delusion. Some see well and clearly and have genuinely long sight, others strain their eyes and may be deceived.

Bear in mind when this occurs the deception is a natural thing, not in the least a matter that should cause surprise, because the guide is not omnipotent.

Man's Path not Inflexible

From this, it would seem that the destiny of man is decided from his birth: that freewill is of no account, that he is born in an iron framework from which he cannot escape. That is not so. Man's path is flexible; it can be altered by himself and his own personal tendencies. The control sees what these tendencies lead to, as far ahead perhaps as ten years, never longer. These desires form a luminous haze around the person concerned, in which his fortunes are written. The future is difficult to read, and is uncertain, but it can be seen, and a good control will make few mistakes. This power is inherent in some controls, not in others. It may be described as an extension of sight, or long sight. Prevision is not a message from the communicator. It must never be regarded as such. It is a message conveyed by a control who has the power of reading the future through the life-mist of the subject.

This is all very obscure, but if you will examine your own evidence, you will find that the prophecy or prediction given by the control never extends to more than ten years ahead, usually it covers a much shorter period, seldom exceeding one year or a few months.

The Inward Eye

Ask your clairvoyant how he sees, and he will reply: "I can't tell you." He cannot understand that inward sight exists which gives him what is called seeing in your sense of the word. "Seeing" is not the best term for it, for it is knowing without learning.

Clairvoyance in all its different branches, must be taken, as it is spoken of, as "second sight." I should define "clairvoyance" as the power to see with the inward eye. It is that which is seen by the inward eye, the impression cannot be explained by the living. You also use the term for the phenomena which frequently occur at public meetings when the control gives the medium a message, either oral or visual, from the communicator. It does not describe the phenomena. Apply the term if you wish, but do not confuse it with prevision.

Clairaudience

Clairaudience may be regarded as a result analogous to automatic messages. Some persons listen and hear words spoken inwardly, others may hear words spoken objectively in the room. These messages heard by the inward ear are not long or voluminous. The hearing and seeing power of the medium is not sustained as a rule for more than a few moments. When the pencil or ouija board are used the messages still come in the same way, but the instrument that records them carries them through much more rapidly than when they are merely heard, the thinking mind is cut off and so they are continuous.

Phenomena at Public meetings

The phenomena at public meetings may be divided into two classes: the people seen, and the people who "build up"[8] as the mediums say. The people seen are subjective to the medium, those who build up are objective. In other words, the people seen with the inner eye and those who "build up" formed out of the ectoplasm by the control. Where the message is clairaudient, it is whispered to the medium by the control or, in some cases, by the communicator, but this is very rare.

---

[8] "Build up" may mislead those who cannot understand how the medium sees the person presented. It is the slow building up of the form from a thin ectoplasm which can only be seen by a sensitive.

Questions and Answers

Q. Question as to prevision – the knowledge of things happening some days later – not only the prevision of someone arriving, but of what he is going to do. Is it correct to suppose that thoughts can be read? (Many experiences of this kind of happenings were quoted by those present.)

A. Yes, it is in a sense so, for the subconscious mind which is active in dreaming, conveys its knowledge to the conscious, can function in an extension of your time and knows what is likely to happen, likely I say, for scarcely any fact in the future is irrevocably fixed. It might not take place, but as a rule it does, and this is, as I tell you, a vision of the inner consciousness that is longer sighted than the ordinary consciousness.

Q. Is the "Inner Eye" the same as the Pineal Gland?

A. No, it is connected with the Pineal Gland but it could not be said to be one and the same thing. The Pineal Gland under certain circumstances can open the "Inner Eye."

10

Psychic Photography

~

I have now to go on to a most important branch of mediumship, much more important than clairvoyance, although clairvoyance is linked up very closely with it. This is psychic photography.

I have tried to explain what seeing with the inward eye is. The psychic photographer has to use this as much and even more than the clairvoyant, for he has to see the image, though in this case unconsciously, and further, to impress that image, with the help of the control, on the ectoplasm.

The Eye of the Soul

I wish to interpolate the remark that the existence of the inward eye has been doubted. None but the Easterns have recognized its power. We from our side know that seated deep in the personality of every living human being, there is a third eye that knows, but that cannot be used except under certain circumstances and by certain persons. This third eye, the Eye of the Soul, is the vehicle by which all knowledge travels from us to you – and by the Eye I mean the mirror that reflects the unknown.

How the Ectoplasm is Emitted

I have tried to make you see how some mediums have the power of loosening and releasing the ectoplasm that is in them. This material varies a great deal in different persons. Some cannot loosen it at all.

In psychic photography ectoplasm is emitted, not in rolling clouds, but as a thin grey mist, and it varies in character in the same medium from day to day. On one occasion he or she sends it out in large masses, while at other times it puffs itself out. Little clouds of it lie about the room. It is unevenly distributed. This explains the difficulty, or rather the many difficulties that lie in the path of the control who must shape his portraits from it.

If the medium does not give out the material generously, the control may have to collect it from different parts of the room, and the exposure may be over before his work is half done, and then the result is a failure.

More Subtle than Materialization

I will try and describe what happens as I see it from my side. It is a much more subtle matter than materialization. It is supremely difficult to make a good psychic photograph. I have said that the medium must see with the inward eye, although unconsciously. The fact is, the inward eye cannot be used satisfactorily except in trance or when the normal sight is absent. The psychic photographer imagines himself in a normal condition. He is in very much the same position as the automatic writer. He cannot use his inward eye well, because images from the normal sight blur his vision. If any face floats before his normal sight, which is not the face of the desired communicator, it will leave its impression on the ectoplasm.

The many so-called failures in psychic photography can be explained in many different ways, but, roughly speaking they can come under three headings:

1. Photographs due to the fact that another sitter has left a strong impression behind.

2. Photographs of spirits who are anxious to use the medium and have pressed in without invitation.

3. Photographs which are connected with the medium himself, friends or relatives, who are possibly nearer to the Earth than the desired communicator, and who can show themselves more easily.

How the Extras are Produced

I want you to understand that there are different forms of psychic photography. You must not imagine that all are produced by the same process. In some cases, where the communicator is accustomed to sittings, and not depressed by the Earth atmosphere, he himself is the operator. But in the majority of cases he cannot act himself, and the control must act for him, that is, he must collect the ectoplasm and with it produce a portrait of the communicator. It is a most difficult task.

Imagine a fluid, gelatinous mass which is alive and which must be moulded into shape, and form the likeness of a spirit not in its own atmosphere, whose shape is vapour-like and transparent. It is almost as impossible as moulding a portrait from flowing water would be, although ectoplasm, as it appears in photographic mediums, has more of the substance of thick cream than water, thick cream possessed of so much vitality that it is an ever-moving mass.

Supersensitive Nature of the Material Used

If the communicator operates, the portrait is produced by him in this way. He must press his face into the substance and when that is done, you almost invariably get the impression of a mask. You must understand that when the living mass is floating on the atmosphere, being supersensitive, it may catch up the thought of the medium or sitter, and then the control, who has to handle it, can no longer mould the portrait, because thought, being a living thing, and entering the living ectoplasm, has left its impress there, and the control cannot impress his idea on it.

A psychic portrait is the expression of an idea. Without the vision of the face of the communicator, the control could not do his work. It is his impression of his subject that is photographed, not the communicator's face as others may see it.

You will perhaps improve matters as time goes on, with regard to this subject, but you can never be sure of your result. I have no hesitation in saying that it is the most difficult form of mediumship. In all other cases the guide can act as control, but here the very fragile nature of the material he has to use makes his results very uncertain. I should say that your only chance of improving conditions for us would be to sit still in a semi-darkened room before the sitting, trying to induce a state of complete passivity. I should have to suggest the same treatment for medium and sitter, and that being usually very difficult, we can only proceed as best we can. The best results occur when the sitter is possessed of psychic power when his or her guide is active, and can assist the guide of the photographer in keeping out intruders.

The Cenotaph Photographs

For psychic photography as it is produced when a mass thought influences, as in the photographs taken at meetings or at the Cenotaph, nothing is accomplished by the communicators. The pictures are all executed by the controls on our side. They are sent especially on such occasions, well equipped for their work. They have an easier task than the control who is working for an individual portrait, for, thought being concentrated from thousands of minds, it is easy to record it. The material given out comes in greater masses, thanks to the concentrated force of many hundreds close together, all sending out their power in one moment and with one idea. It steadies the ectoplasm, in fact it practically receives only one idea, and the control who has the portraits ready can impress them on it without much difficulty.

You must not call these portraits, moulds. There is a prevalent idea that our controls make masks, as a sculptor would, and press these into the ectoplasm. Mould is not the word. The control has the idea of the face in his mind. He has let this idea sink into himself so that he can reproduce it in the ectoplasm without a sitter on our side. All the Cenotaph portraits are the ideas the controls have formed of individual faces.

Symbols

Then at meetings you sometimes get photographs of crosses, wreaths, banners, all kinds of symbols. In such cases, the controls have worked through thoughts in the minds of certain psychic individuals present. They have collected these thoughts and have produced a symbol from them. At a memorial meeting for those who have fallen in the war, you will probably get a cross, which Christian symbol is in the minds of many – a wreath, or several wreaths, which again are symbols of the dead, or banners, which denote victory. Take them as thoughts gathered from the audience, they are nothing more.

Lastly before I leave the subject, I should like to remind you that photographs can be taken of living individuals who are not present. If the camera records such portraits, they are photographs of the thoughts in the minds of the sitters present where the photograph is taken, or of a person deeply interested in the photograph or place where the picture is taken, and who projects his thoughts there.

This will go far to prove my contention that psychic photographs are never portraits of the actual face of a discarnate human being. They are photographs of a thought in the control's mind, or they may be portraits of the actual faces passed through a thick sheet, which makes them appear like masks. This is an attempt to sum up the subject, but much has to be left unsaid.

Questions and Answers

Q. Question with reference to Skotographs – i.e. results obtained on plates not exposed in the camera.

A. Skotographs are produced in exactly the same way as the ordinary psychic photograph, the results are seldom as good as those taken with the camera because the mechanism is cramped and the power finds it much more difficult to act. For experimental purposes the skotograph is a valuable testimony.

Q. Can you tell us anything about colour photography?

A. I have said nothing about that here because it is a comparatively new experiment on our side.

Q. But we have obtained wonderful results with Mrs. Deane.[9]

A. Yes, excellent when you have the right control, but we cannot always capture the right one, and then they tend to become failures. The plate doesn't matter. It is the control who matters, and very few have made an art of this.

Q. We are told that so many on your side are interested in psychic photography, why?

A. Because they want to give a visual impression somehow to those who are left behind. After the soul returns and realizes it is invisible to those who are on Earth, the desire to show itself is intense. They know that seeing is believing.

Q. Can you explain screen markings on some of the "extras"? (This question was answered by Mrs. Dowden's Control, Johannes.)

---

[9] See *Faces of the Living Dead*. Stead Library.

A. There are so many different methods adopted to obtain results wanted. Some faces are not so easy to take into the mind. Markings are never present unless the memory of the face is incorrect or merely partial, then the face is constructed bit by bit, and these markings occur.

11

Hauntings

~

The Common Ghost

I had not exhausted the many forms of mediumship which exist, but before I describe another I should like to tell you how I saw, what you living people call the common ghost, the ghost that is not evoked through any special medium.

I was put on this track through the materializations I had seen. I suddenly remembered a certain house in which I had been told hauntings occurred, and immediately I resolved to get the right explanation. I was surprised by what met me there, but not surprised on one point. I had always believed that it was impossible that the spirits of the dead really survived in the places in which they lived, going automatically through the scenes of their lives night after night for years after they had died.

The house in question had been familiar to me from my early youth. I thought of it at once, and found myself there at night, at the time I remembered these hauntings had occurred. You gather from all I have said that by this time I was becoming familiar with the atmosphere of the Earth, and that now I hardly felt the oppression on my return to your world. You are right, but I was totally unprepared for what I found in this haunted house. I found an atmosphere there, which might justly be described as a storm.

Not a storm of wind, although a cold wind blew with great violence through the house, not wind, no, but a storm of emotion, a hurricane, I should say, for it was so violent I felt I might be gathered into the maelstrom, and was actually afraid at first to enter. But curiosity conquered fear. I plunged into it, and no one was there after all, nothing but this living storm of thought. It was like some great engine that every few hours puffed out great volumes of smoke which were capable of taking shapes, shapes which seemed alive, but were in reality only dreams of hate, revenge, love or grief.

Vapours without Light or Soul within

The storm seemed confined to the four walls of the house. In this case hauntings occurred only inside, and the moment I entered, I felt as though I had been thrown about into a boiling sea and was being tossed about in it by an unseen hand. At first I saw nothing, then after a time my vision cleared, and I saw forms coming out of the mass of steam, coming out of it in human shape. They seemed to be alive, except that as I saw them they were only vapours. There was no light or soul within them. They made their round as their human prototypes had done in their lifetimes, and became part of the vapour again when their task was accomplished.

Communication Possible but Rare

I asked myself, "Are these ghosts?"[10] Then what about the ghosts that speak or send messages to their friends or about their belongings? Are they the same as these phantoms? This was made clear to me later but as I am now on the subject, I may as well explain it here. When a strong desire to communicate exists in the human soul, and

------

[10] Please note that the word "ghost" is correctly applied to these emotional forms which have a mere semblance of reality.

when there is no available medium, and when the emotion preceding death has been overwhelming, strong enough to leave a steam engine behind it, the soul may use the inanimate form produced out of the steam as its garment, and may be able to impress the brain of the person for whom it is intended. Only overwhelming emotion would give the soul courage to do this. It is naturally rare, and it only occurs where the message is extremely urgent.

I was so upset by this experience, that for a time I could neither analyse nor explain it. I did not fully understand it until it was made quite clear to me that the human soul cannot communicate with the sphere below it except through a special instrument, a medium in fact, and the case I have mentioned is an extreme one of emotional hauntings.

Hauntings in Open Spaces

There are many different degrees of haunting. It may be a gentle, or audible impression. In such a case the haunting is actually beneficent, it increases the favourable atmosphere of the house. I must however, go into the strange and unaccountable phantoms that can be seen in open spaces, even in the streets, and often where there are woods and trees. The existence of such phantoms cannot be doubted, but the cause of them, is a puzzle even to us who have gone one step further than you have.

These, so far as I can tell, are due to three different causes:

(*1*) Where a tragic event has taken place, such as a murder. That is easily accounted for, passion and remorse would not wither easily, they would return either with ferocity or with wailing regret, and hover round the scene of the tragedy.

(2) Hauntings appearing in connection with a body of persons who inhabited a building now destroyed, who were immured from the world. The sites of prisons, or a dungeon would preserve such emotions, or the site of a monastery or convent

where suppressed desire would have a chance of expression long after the human souls had left the scene.

This is the commonest form of haunting in an open space and the emotions left behind being earthbound would preserve an automatic life for a very long time. These hauntings can be very dangerous, because as a rule they are connected with suppressed sex.

The hauntings in the woods or under trees are different from the other two instances I have quoted. Hauntings connected with the woods are psychometric. If great emotions, or even lesser emotions have taken place in a wood, or in a place where there are many trees, the trees would soak them in, and give them out as they breathe. Nothing that lives has the same power of preserving thought and emotion as a tree. It possesses a most marvellous psychometric power.

It is an octopus that sucks the thoughts and feelings of those who are much in its company.

Power of Emotion on Objects

I want to link this up with another subject, to explain that an emotion if it is strong enough, leaves itself on everything that is worn or touched by the emotional subject. Emotion is a living thing. It is as much alive as ectoplasm, but with this difference – that emotion comes straight from the soul, while ectoplasm is partly a physical substance. A ring worn in the time of Noah, having endured the ravages of the flood, would retain the picture produced by fear of water for all the ages it endures.

Emotion sets up a life of its own after it leaves the soul, and becomes a living entity separated from the parent. I shall not enlarge on this further, for my object in writing this present book is to speak of my own experiences, not to explain the living can experience for themselves.

Dangers of being in a Haunted House

Before closing this chapter I want to emphasize that it is most undesirable for the average human being to live in a haunted house. The atmosphere of emotion may infect the Earth inhabitants. They are likely to be disturbed by depressing or distressing emotions, but they are not often in physical danger. The popular idea that spiritual presences are so evil that they may or can inflict physical hurt on the living is unfounded so far as the souls of those who have departed are concerned, but they are not unfounded where the way has been left open to great forces of hate or venom. These forces have the power to take on themselves a physical and concrete life of their own. They are not dangerous in themselves, but if they are backed up by great natural forces they are highly dangerous, and can even kill or hurt the body, the soul they cannot touch.

The Vampire and the Werewolf

This fact accounts for the tales of vampires, which take on themselves, the shape of birds – the symbol of the bird of prey. Behind the emotion there is a natural force for evil which uses and manipulates the emotion for its own ends, that is the simplest way to express it.

Don't dismiss the tales of the vampire and the werewolf as mere foolish prattle, for there is truth behind both beliefs.

Questions and Answers

Q. Would a psychic get the thoughts from the trees?

A. Yes, probably very vividly, but psychics respond to different forms of environment. Some respond to water, some to trees, some to open spaces. It is all bound up with their astrological aspects.

Q. Can you explain the Werewolf?

A. If a human being lends himself to dangerous and evil practices, in other words, if he opens the doors, the accumulated terror of his people may produce the effect of an animal, then he may under certain conditions, assume the animal form of the nation's fear. He enters into the animal completely. He changes into an animal.

Q. Can hauntings ever materialize?

A. Yes, certainly if the emotion has been abnormal.

Q. How is it that some hauntings are heard only at special times?

A. Anniversaries will cause this, atmospheric conditions and astrological conditions, and it may occur at the waning of the moon.

Q. How is it that hauntings have occurred, and voices have been heard in quite new houses?

A. No place invites wanderers so much as a new house. The house which has no hauntings or memories is open to the wanderers. They will enter and play there.

Q. Are ordinary (non-psychic) people safe in haunted houses?

A. Yes, so long as they do not allow their thoughts to dwell on hauntings. On the other hand if the hauntings are the result of evil deeds, and evil thoughts, it is not desirable for people to live there.

Q. How is it that in freeing a haunted house mediums get in touch with the actual spirits?

A. I think I can show you how it is. The souls of the dead which have left these ghosts behind may be summoned, but that is unusual. The fact is, that, as a ring or a book left on your table helps to summon a communicator, so the shells of emotion which contain part of the personality can summon them if used by a medium.

Q. Having been summoned, and having come into touch with a medium, can the soul disperse the emotion left behind?

A. Yes, it can take that part of itself away, and drop it in the halfway house between the Earth and the next sphere. The Theosophists' "astral" might explain this.

12

The Poltergeist

I have not dealt so far with the phenomena commonly called poltergeist hauntings. These are not uncommon, and are always annoying, and, at times, amusing. They attach themselves to persons rather than places, and, as a rule, are temporary. The explanation often is, that these entities are caught in the astral web, and having no real existence for the time being, amuse themselves by returning to Earth, and playing with human beings who are fully alive. They have no direct intention any more than an animal or a small child would have.

It is, as I have said, a misfortune to be caught in the astral web, because it delays progress, and knowledge, and while human souls are there, they are living in a dream existence, they cannot be said to be alive. These poltergeist hauntings give them an existence that seems more real to them. In fact, these hauntings need never be feared, they are not malicious though they may annoy. They may attack the automatist, seize the pencil, before anyone from our sphere could get hold of the pencil, and impersonate our communicators. In fact they are responsible for most of the unfortunate mistakes which occur in automatic writing. They attack two forms of mediumship, table and writing, including the Ouija board.

They do not attack trance, because the medium is out of the body, and they could not deceive him or her. In the case of voice mediumship, they can invade if the controls are not watchful, but they seldom do. They have existence apart from the astral, and it is difficult for a guide to expel them. It can be done by the use of certain signs, and by the invocation of certain powers, but even then the expulsion is temporary.

Apparitions: What are They?

Before leaving this subject I should like to say a few words about the apparitions or warnings, which occur immediately before death, at the time of death or immediately after death. The apparitions, I am now speaking of, visual ones, are invariably the projection of thought. They are the visible form of a vibration.

If a dying person thinks intently of some special friends the thought sent out is so intense, so material, that its vibration can create an actual picture. Those after death are the commonest. The dying seldom know how near death they are. After death, for a moment, the spirit realizes almost automatically what has happened, and sends out thought to some beloved friend at a distance, this thought vibrates so intensely that it creates its own image. The act of dying, the change which is taking place and which sets the soul free, excites it and gives it power to make this temporary appearance. These apparitions rise from concentrated thought, projected, or from the state of intoxication of the soul, it scintillates, as it were, and may become visible to many persons at the same moment. The dying, or dead, may be said to be present in such cases through the intensity of their thoughts.

The Double

The double which is occasionally seen by the living is not an apparition of the same kind. It is an escape of the inner envelope of the personality at such times as the person seen, is asleep, unconscious, or delirious.

This apparition which you call the "Double" can be produced in two different ways, when the subject is unconscious it can escape, as I have said, taking on itself the appearance of its possessor, even including the clothes worn at the time, or it may escape when its possessor is conscious, but when the mind is passive and inactive, but these cases are less frequent than those during which the subject is asleep.

Questions and Answers

Q. When the apparition of a dying person remains for a long time, as is said to have happened in some cases, would that be accomplished through concentrated thought power?

A. In such cases the deep concentration of thought would keep the image there. If the disembodied soul held the image of some beloved person in its consciousness the apparition might remain some time.

13

Apports

~

The next thing that I investigated was the form of mediumship where apports occur. I had no intention to operate myself, and soon I was convinced that all the work done in that direction is the work of the medium's control. I have found no instance where it was due to the operation of the communicator, although it often professes to be so. I shall tell you about my first experience. This was at a sitting where two things were produced, a flower, and a small silver brooch. The first of these, the flower, was laid on the séance table about three quarters of an hour after the sitting begun. The brooch at the end of two hours.

How it is Done

At this sitting I watched the control operate with great interest. He fetched the rose, a red one, from a garden at some distance away, and proceeded to dematerialize it. That is, he took the atoms of which it was composed, separated them without injuring the life that was in the flower, which of course was entirely detached from the material part. He dropped these atoms through the brain centres of the medium. First the soul of the flower entered involuntarily, finding a hiding place for itself in the brain after it was divested of its material substance. Having filtered through the brain, the control rehabilitated the flower soul, and laid the finished work on the table.

It was beautifully and quickly done. The medium did not seem to be conscious of the process. I watched a similar experiment with the brooch, which having a very inferior form of life, was easier to put together, or rebuild, after it had passed through the brain of the medium.

With regard to dematerialization and apports, I want my readers to understand that my experience is very limited, and further, though I saw the guide go and fetch the flower and the brooch, I was in no position to say how he scattered the atoms of which they were composed. I am convinced, however, that only guides can do this. People in my sphere would be unable to do it, and further, I am convinced that these experiments will always be rare, for very few guides interest themselves in such things.

I will explain exactly what I saw. I went with the guide to a garden not far from the séance room, where he plucked the rose. He did not dematerialize the stalk to do this, it seemed to be plucked as any of you would pluck it. He then carried it to the séance and dematerialized it before he entered the room. This transit was accomplished in an instant, so that if any living person had seen the rose plucked, in his measurement of time the flower would be carried to the house, dematerialized and constructed again in the space of about one second. I had few opportunities of watching these experiments. It was not easy to find a medium who could do them. I found it more enlightening to attend less material forms of sittings.

Levitation and Telekinesis?

Levitation is regarded quite rightly as a form of psychic phenomena, but it has not been recognized on your side that there are various forms of levitation the causes of which are different.

Daniel Home

Let me first take a case such as Daniel Home, where the levitation was involuntary. He being a superfine psychic, was tuned up to such a point that he could, without the help of his guides, raise his inner soul body and carry with it his physical body. I will explain myself. When Home rose into the air and floated out of one window and into another, it was a superhuman feat. His psychic body being infinitely stronger than the physical was able to carry the physical with it. That is one rare and wonderful form of levitation. It is seldom seen. In fact it is almost unique in Western Europe. In the East adepts are able to do the same thing, but it is the result of long and painful training.

Crawford Experiments

That form of levitation has nothing in common with the raising of a table as in the Crawford experiments.[11] In those experiments the medium had to be reinforced by other sitters. She would not have been able to raise the table alone. She did it with the help of others, who with her formed a strong lever, which held it in the air not for a moment only, but for many moments. The medium projected this strong lever from the solar plexus, in the form of a wide bar, which had greater strength than a steel bar of the same dimensions, while the sitters each contributed a strong thread of ectoplasm.

Now I come to the levitation of objects. Again it can occur in two different ways. First let us take a case where an object in the room appears to rise of its own accord.

In such a case the medium gives out involuntarily a bar or lever such as was used in the Crawford experiments with this difference, that the raising of the object is unintentional.

When the objects are raised by holding hands over them there is an entirely different factor at work. In that case there is a magnetic quality in the medium which can attract such objects.

---

[11] See Crawford's *Experiments in Psychic Science*. Stead Library.

Where this power is present, you will find that certain objects will make an approach, while others will not. It is the same quality exactly as the power of a magnet to attract metals.

Dowsing

The power of finding metals and water underground is a quality certain persons possess, and it is rightly considered a psychic quality, for it is magnetic, as the magnetism that draws the scissors or knife in cases of telekinesis. The power of finding water is inherent in persons who have certain elements in their horoscope. The same remark applies to the finding of metals. The influence above and outside the Earth draws the influence within. It is not often that one individual can find both water and metals. Dowsers for water are much more common than metal dowsers, for the simple reason that so many people are born under the Aquarius sign, but it does not follow that because you are born under that sign you have the dowsing power. It is only under certain circumstances when planetary influences are grouped favourably, that this power is present. In neither case, that of dowsing for water or for metals is there any external agency at work, no guide or control assists the process. It comes automatically from the individual who possesses the power.

The Stigmata

Another manifestation that may puzzle the public is what is called the power of producing the stigmata. Now here again there is no external agency at work.

No guide or saint on our side inspires the production of the wounds. The power is latent in the individual. If that individual concentrated on producing the number ten on his hand with the same enthusiasm and faith as he produces the wounds, the number "ten" would appear. It means abnormal power of concentration, nothing more.

Questions and Answers

Q. Do you mean that the physical atoms are separated and then passed through the walls of the room?

A. Yes the physical atoms have to be separated and then passed through the walls of the room, which is a simple matter, while the spiritual part of the flower, or in a smaller sense of the metal is passed through the brain centres of the medium.

Q. What is the object of passing them through the brain centres?

A. The object is that when the physical atoms are separated from the psychic, the psychic would lose its individuality and become part of the group flower soul, or soul of the metal.

Q. How would you explain the cases when saints have been levitated?

A. These levitations mean that the spiritual or psychic body is twice the size of the physical and therefore able to carry it along. Eventually the whole would be permeated with psychic power and physical atoms burnt up.

Q. How is it that the power to dowse is often intermittent?

A. It would vary with the aspects of the moon. If you have the opportunity you can verify this.

14

How to Approach Communication

~

Hints from the other side

It may help those on Earth who wish to communicate with us, to give them our side of the question. How our friend on Earth approaches us? Can we give him a few useful hints and suggestions? Yes, undoubtedly we can. Many of you do not seem to understand our position in the least. First let me emphasize the most important point for us.

Living not Dead

Try to think of us as the living, not the dead. That word "dead" should be eliminated from the vocabulary of people who wish to reach the sphere above them. Not only should you call us the living, but, in spite of the fact that you cannot see us, you must feel that we are actually there. We are more alive than you are, as a matter of fact, and nothing daunts us so much as your attitude, if you fail to feel our presence at a sitting.

Please consider what I say and act on it to the full extent of your power. I can remember my own sensations when I first tried to reach the "other world", and I sympathize with those who find it difficult to feel that we are living, but you can overcome that difficulty, and if you are to have good results, you must, that is the first essential.

Honest Scepticism Appreciated

I do not quarrel in the least with honest scepticism. In fact the subject of psychic investigation would have no honourable standing but for the honest sceptics. We do not object to scepticism. We are just as rational as you are. We are most sympathetic with cautious sitters, and ready to help them, but if their attitude is one of suspicion – if they treat us as they would pickpockets, for instance – it retards results. Therefore I beg you to give us a chance. Think of us as living human souls who are eager to reach you.

Attitude of Sympathetic Expectancy

Criticize us by all means, but keep the criticism back until the sitting is over. Let your attitude be that of sympathetic expectancy. Do not give the medium suggestions, it is not helpful to us. We vary, as much as you do, some of us are quick on the "uptake", others are slower. When changing the medium, new conditions appertain, which may make the commencement of a sitting difficult. So please have mercy on us and do not be too impatient.

How to Approach Communication

Is it wise to consult one medium only, and to have a long series of sittings with him or her? That depends on the communicator. Some of us here are not adventurous, and prefer the same guide and the same atmosphere. Others do far better if the medium is changed often.

Always in the beginning consult three different kinds of mediums. We find out in that way, which methods suit us best.

Fatal to begin Sittings under Wrong Conditions

I should like to explain that the sitter should, when possible, come to the sitting in a quiet frame of mind, not hurried and not thinking of engagements, and not when any form of illness is troubling him or her. It is fatal to begin sittings under wrong conditions. Often grief-stricken persons come to their first interview in a disturbed and highly emotional frame of mind, which makes it as difficult for us, as the most sneering doubter would. Of course emotion under such circumstances is natural, but, when possible, it should be kept under control until the results have been obtained.

We need Response

Please remember also, that all the response you give, helps us, draws response from us. Think of it in this way. Your brother who was your dearest and nearest relative, has been in Australia for thirty years. He returns, and you meet again. Would you stand by silently if he talked to you? If you treated him in this way, would he continue to try to get some response from you? No, he would probably cease his effort. On our side we sometimes feel that it is not the Earth inhabitants who have changed, it is we ourselves who have become more emotional, who understand the value of love more, than when we were in the body, and who wither when we find no response from the sphere below us.

Advice to Scientific Investigators

Now, a word to the scientific investigators, I want to help them. Let me first deal with the mediumship that is called physical. This is more difficult than mental mediumship, for in such cases the medium is subjected to a far greater strain and danger. The manifestations that are given through such mediums, are usually put forward by scientists on our side, who want to give proof of supernormal phenomena to their collaborators in the sphere below.

Materialization a Highly Specialized Game

In fact, mediumship for materialization might be described as a highly specialized game. You will never get proof of human survival in this way which will satisfy the emotions. In fact it cannot be said that, except in the case of completely materialized forms, there is any proof of survival given at these sittings. I should not discourage such sittings, quite the contrary, I look on them as one of our most useful advertisements, but they never can have the emotional value of mental mediumship.

Doubt, the Cause of Fraud

Now let me leave the physical mediums, but with a warning. The scientific investigators should, of course, eliminate fraud as far as they possibly can, but their attitude to the medium is all important. Set up doubt in the medium's mind of your belief in his honesty and you yourself have created a condition which will easily lead him to either subconscious, or conscious fraud. His passivity is disturbed. He is no longer a channel, but an instrument that cannot be used efficiently any longer, because of the atmosphere that you have created.

No Result, No Response

When scientists investigate mental mediumship, the conditions are still more difficult. Even in trance mediumship, some response from the sitter is needed.

It is true the medium is in trance and is alive to the fact that no response is made to any statement given by the guide, and so the sitting will not continue satisfactorily. The medium's subconscious mind will be sufficiently awake to turn the results into a new and more general channel, if the sitter remains entirely unresponsive. Again, in a voice sitting, all who have attended these, notice that results cease if no response is given from your side. Not that the communicator is unaware of your presence, not that he does not see you. You are closed against him. He is battering on a door that will not open, and so he retires.

Advice to Professional Mediums

What I am about to say is addressed to mediums, and by mediums I mean those persons who have decided to devote their time to giving sittings, and who earn their living in this way. I should like first to address a word to the public with regard to professional mediumship. It is often said by persons who have not considered the matter sensibly, that mediums who possess what is commonly called a gift, should not accept money for the results they are able to give. This is an absurd contention. In all professions, medicine, church, the law, those persons who are able to do the work accept money for the exercise of their powers.

The Sensitive – a Super-Human Being

Why should the channel by which you can reach the other world be an exception? It would tell against your results if your mediums were not paid. They would necessarily allow their powers to lapse and would not be ready to serve you, except when their own inclinations suggested it. I should like you to regard the medium as a person who should be cared for and supported, preserved as the vestals were preserved, as priests and priestesses, whose importance cannot be overestimated. I wish to emphasize this point and I hope that my readers will help me to spread the knowledge, that the sensitive is a superhuman being.

Attitude to Guide all Important

Now I address the sensitives from my side of the question. How can they best help us to communicate satisfactorily? First their attitude to their own guides is all important. The medium should not be subservient to the guide, should not be idolatrous, in his or her attitude. The guide should be regarded as a collaborator and friend, and should be taken into the confidence of the medium as much as possible. No medium can state confidently that he knows his guide through and through. The guide's personality may be dominant or the reverse. At times guides are inclined to dominate the situation far too much. The medium should aim at an even collaboration with the guide. This can be attained, in almost all cases, if the medium preserves the right attitude. The medium must preserve a placid condition of mind, and to attain this, the desire to produce results must be put aside. This is most difficult for the professional medium, and this desire has produced almost all the fraud that has ever been connected with the subject. It is not just, to contend that fraud is a desire to make more money.

Fraud caused through Nervous Tension

At times, and with the lower types of mediums, it is, but the larger number of cases where fraud has been detected, are those where the medium's anxiety and perhaps the sitter's aloofness, has produced a state of nervous tension in the subconscious, and almost unconsciously the medium resorts to fraud.

So my best advice to a professional medium is, establish an even relationship with your guide. Let him do his work, and you do yours, which is to allow your mind to hang in a state of complete passivity and put away from you any desire to make the sitting successful. This advice is easy to carry out in most cases with the trance medium, but extremely difficult where the medium is fully conscious. Conscious mediums can only attain the right condition through long experience and much practice of their powers.

Change and Recreation Essential

Now one word more. Mediums should lead lives which isolate their work from their other occupations. They should not concentrate on the sittings they give except at the times they give them. It is not well to talk continually about the subject in their leisure hours. We want them fresh, if they are to serve us well. They must have change and recreation if their work is to be well done. They should not attend meetings or occupy themselves with psychic work, except when they are giving sittings.

Advice to Amateur Mediums

Now I shall address a word to amateur mediums who get their own results at home. The first essential is patience. Hurried results can never be satisfactory. Those who hope to reach their communicators truly and fully in a short time, will meet with grave disappointments. Let us take the case of Ouija board sittings, which are the commonest for the amateur. If the result comes rapidly, or without the help of a guide or control, the messages are likely to become confused, and even false after a time. This at once suggests demoniac intervention and the sittings cease, and the whole subject is given a wrong aspect by these people.

Go Slowly. Guide's assistance Essential

If they understood the conditions on our side they would see that their own facility has lead them to these pitfalls. They should not leap to conclusions as to the nature of the interference. Until the guide has appeared, they have been working without a safeguard. All those who work as amateurs, should devote a considerable time to discovering who their guides are. They should ask definitely for their help, and refuse to go on until they appear. Even this will not safeguard them. Until they have tested the guides who come to them, and have given them a chance to get a firm hold of their conditions they should not dismiss their communications as unsound and impossible. We must demand at least a full year's test from them, before we can create a clear channel for communication.

Testing Guides

How can guides be tested? They can only be tested by using them for at least six months, and then taking the average of what has been right, and what wrong. Even then the sitters may not have got into touch with the deeper guides. They may be dealing with a light upper stratum of the guide's personality, who, as a whole, cannot function at once.

Universal Mediumship: Is it advisable?

There is an idea afloat, that universal mediumship should be possible, in fact that we should aim at bringing this about, that training for mediumship should be part of the curriculum of every child's education, that as the cultivation of mediumship becomes universal, it will also be hereditary, handed on from father to son. I should like to remind people, who are inclined to push this doctrine, that universal mediumship is a complete impossibility. I, too, look forward to psychic training being part of every child's education, but I do not look forward to having mediums in every walk of life. The objections are: first that many persons are quite unfitted for mediumship cannot open themselves to impressions from our side, and moreover their occupations interfere with the cultivation of psychic power. Mediums must give up their time, I will not say their entire time, but a great part of it, to their vocation. It will not do to have other interests interfere. When we try to communicate they must be free from cares as far as possible, and they must lead a quiet and regular life.

Need for Specialization

To the end of all time mediumship must be specialized. The tool must be sharpened for the work it has to do and must preserve that sharpness. It would indeed be an impossible world, if mediumship became a general thing, if say eight out of every ten people cultivated it, it would weaken results all round, but as fortunately this is impossible, we need not waste time discussing it.

Subtleties of Communication

Subtleties must always be taken into consideration even in the simplest and most straightforward sitting. You cannot lay down broad rules that will make things easy when the thought conveyed, depends on a tiny and very delicate vibration which has to be translated by the medium. There are endless difficulties for us, as there are for you, but we intend to overcome them, and, with time and patience, we shall do so to a great extent. I want to emphasize that no sitting is simple, that in every case in which you receive a message from our side, there has been the will to make it clear and straightforward, but the means are not always at our disposal, because of the trouble we have in establishing complete harmony with you. Even with the same communicator, who has been accustomed to the same medium, sitter and guide, the message must vary, for so many factors are at work. This must be always the case. I do not see how we can assure conditions for you, for where weather, health, and the emotions of two persons are factors for and against our success, the medium scarcely comes into the field more than the sitter. The sitter's attitude is all important, his mind interacts on the medium's mind, and through it, on the communicator's, thus it is clear that an inactive sitter, who does not use his mind for the purpose, cannot hope for results. If sympathy and emotion are not given to us we cannot convey feelings.

Questions and Answers

Q. Would you like to see circles in every home?

A. I should not at all approve of it, it would mean that the subject was pulled downwards by untutored persons who would attract unworthy entities. It would not be advisable from any point of view except that of scientific investigation, or for the purpose of making experiments. I hope I do not repress those who are enthusiastic, by saying this, but this is my opinion.

Q. Do you approve of circles for home communication?

A. Yes if worked on a common-sense basis.

15

Communications from Spheres far Beyond

~

How it is Achieved

I have dealt earlier in this little book, with communication between the sphere I am now in and the one above, but I have not dealt with a subject which must interest many seekers. Can we communicate with far distant spheres and reach the mighty dead who have passed on in former ages? The answer to this question is yes, with modifications. Let us choose some important person and discuss the possibility of getting in touch with him. Let us take St. Paul for instance, who has recently been sending messages to the Earth sphere. Is it possible that a medium on Earth can get into direct communication with one who has been on our side for so many hundreds of years? No, is the reply to that question and without any modification whatever. It would be absolutely impossible to have any message of the nature of these that I am giving you now from the higher spheres.

Groups of Amanuenses

However messages can be sent under certain circumstances. If there is a purpose behind the sending of the message, it will be made possible to convey it. The higher spheres, and now I am speaking of the three highest, cannot communicate directly with the lower spheres, but they can communicate through assistants and guides. If the message is of any real importance the whole scheme is organized. A group of amanuenses is formed on each of the spheres below the one on which St. Paul is, and these secretaries convey the messages to the spheres below.

Why is it necessary to send it in sections? Because it is a fatiguing form of communication for these messengers or guides, they take it in turn, each member of a group doing a few pages at a time. This form of communication scarcely ever occurs, unless there is some important purpose behind it. Mere curiosity would not draw a message from Shakespeare for instance, but, on the other hand, if there were some mystery to be cleared up, or if he wanted to inspire or help a dramatist, he could do so with the help of the amanuenses in the spheres below him. The higher the sphere the more fatiguing and difficult it is to send down accurate and correct messages. Confusion occurs chiefly because so many are concerned in its transmission.

Coloured and Altered in Transmission

I can speak directly to you and give you my message as it was born in my own mind, but the message you get from St. Paul will not come to you as it was born in the mind of the saint. It has to be reshaped by every amanuensis who works in the spheres below his, and, as on Earth a rumour loses or gains in the spreading of it, so these messages lose or gain in the elaborate process of sending them.

Interesting and useful information has been sent to the Earth in this way from distant spheres, but not often, and in many cases when it has purported to be truthful and evidential, it has passed through the hands of amanuenses who may be imaginative, and much has grown out of the original thought. This applies to several books which purport to give record of the life of Christ. In no case has the true story come down to the world. Emotion and imagination play such a part in the sending of the message, that it invariably loses or gains and has only a portion of the original thought in it.

If you are on the fourth sphere you can get to the fifth, but though I can get to the fifth, messages from that sphere would not be as clear and satisfactory as messages from the sphere above my own – there is a break.

I want to show the difficulties on our side. When messages from distant spheres are sent, it is not the fault of the amanuenses that they have grown or shrunk in the sending. The organization is so difficult that we are not to blame for mistakes. In every message of like kind there is a modicum of truth.

16

What and Who are our Guides and Controls?

~

What part does the control or guide, play at a sitting? Of what nature is his work? Where does he come from, and why and how is he summoned? These are very natural questions, and even from our side it is difficult to answer them clearly.

Remember, that they are as invisible to us, as they are to you, except when they help us at a sitting, then we are not only conscious of their presence, but we actually see them, sometimes singly, sometimes as a group, but they do not take any visible part in our daily life.

You may ask, are they human? Have they ever inhabited the Earth, and if so, what calls them back? Yes, they are intensely human. They lived on the Earth hundreds of years ago. This applies to most cases, not all, they belong to groups. Some of them work as a group, and control as a group. Others as individuals, but these have a group control behind them which has the full experience of the seven spheres, which they have not.

The Group Control

The group control I shall call the guides. The group has a philosophy of its own. Mediums who are controlled by a group, produce an entirely different type of work from those who are controlled by an individual. The controls, or guides must have passed through the seven periods of their existence, they must have travelled through the seven spheres. Then they are free to choose, whether they will pass into the unknown, or whether they prefer to keep their individuality, in which case, they must work in one, or several of the spheres below them. They may aptly be called the Teachers, or Masters, for they have had the certainty of eternal life forced on them, through their varied experiences.

First I must explain, that the control or guide, does not take part in the life of his medium, unless he is specially asked to do so. The medium is an efficient instrument, used for his work, he has no desire to interfere in his or her daily life, which interests him but little in his stage of development. When the medium is conscious of the interference of his, or her control in daily life, the control is using the power for his own ends, and not out of consideration of the medium's interests.

The Individual Control

The word "guide" has been used, without the full understanding of the function of these older spiritual beings. The control can choose his own type of work. If he is to work in a group, he will teach his own understanding and philosophy of the Universe. If he is to do work as an individual, he takes lesser tasks. He probably chooses to cement evidence of eternal life, in a way that occurs to him. He takes a medium who has a sense of, and interest in, detail. He is ready to place before his medium at all the sittings, symbols which represent the idea he wishes to convey, that is he shows them, through the brain centres of the medium, for as he occupies these, he is so much merged in the medium, that they become one soul for the moment.

The best method for the individual control is trance, because here the conscious mind, being perfectly passive, the inner eye of the medium, sees the symbols clearly, because the control is able to enter the brain centres. The memories of the communicator are reflected in the mirror by the control, in shapes and patterns. To force the mirror to reflect accurately, the medium's subconscious mind must learn a new language from the control, must learn the meaning of those symbols held up for reflection. In the course of time the mirror reflects accurately, it has, in fact, learnt the language of symbols.

Training His Instrument

The control's part is both of instructor and operator. You can see how important the development of the medium is. During the period of training, the control is at work all the time, burnishing and polishing his instrument. Instructing his medium, tentatively at first, but systematically and firmly as time goes on. Sometimes the control does not appear, until he is summoned. Sometimes, if he finds the instrument suitable, he will force it to respond to his desire to use it. The control, as I said, thinks little of the medium's private interests, but he does consider the medium's health. The experienced control will not operate when the medium is ill, or disturbed in mind, because he knows that the apparatus is out of order, or, when in the presence of a person who might be physically dangerous.

First let me take the person who has been in a house with hauntings in it, which can attach themselves to a psychic. Of what nature are such hauntings, and how can they get hold of a living person? These hauntings are often left in a house, or a room by someone who is living in your world. When evil has been done in that place, it can attach itself to a sensitive if the door is opened, and it will not let go, even when the sensitive leaves the room. By the sensitive, I do not mean the medium. Any person who is capable of contacting these conditions, must have psychic power of his or her own, and such a person will be dangerous to the medium, who is a more powerful sensitive. The hauntings will be pretty sure to travel from one to the other.

Then certain persons, who are of doubtful character, carry with them influences which can attach themselves to a medium temporarily. These influences have contacted through the misconduct of someone in close proximity to sensitive.

Such influences are highly dangerous, but in all these cases, if the guide is thoroughly experienced, he can either drive away evil influence, or he can refuse to make any connection.

Now this leads us to a very interesting point, what do I mean by connection? By this I mean that the four, who are essential to the sitting – the medium, sitter, communicator and control must tune in. If that does not occur, there is no possibility of communication. In all forms of mediumship it is the same. Until the four are attuned, there can be no results.

Most of the cases in which evil things attach themselves to psychics, are those where some abuse of sex has occurred. Sex is a fundamental thing in all our lives. It is the root of all that IS.[12] Its abuse is dangerous to a degree that is quite misunderstood on your side. The active evil that the abuse creates, is one of the great difficulties that come in the way of communication. It is ever ready to catch on when it gets the chance. The control who works for trance condition has an easy time compared with those, who work for voice, or even writing. He has his instrument completely at his disposal. He has not the difficulty of a mental apparatus that is living its own life, and using its own thoughts, apart from the pressure he wants to get through. In fact, the individual control who forces himself on a trance medium, and uses that medium wisely, gets a better condition than any other form of mediumship. He cannot put his philosophy through as a group can, but he gets his details clear cut.

All Controls Part of a Larger Body

You will understand through what I have said that controls work in different ways, and for different purposes. Although I speak of some of these spiritual presences working individually, I intend you

[12] See note in Appendix

to accept the fact, that they are part of a larger body. As the soul ascends the ladder of the spheres, it tends to merge itself more and more, into other spirits congenial to itself, who strengthen it on its journey. When the seventh sphere is reached, the controls appear as group souls. In that sphere they have no separate individuality. When they descend to any of the lower spheres, they can detach themselves from their group, if they wish to do so. Let me give you an instance. Johannes works with his group at all times, he does not detach himself as an individual. But Feda does, she detaches herself, and works entirely apart from her group, and interests herself in detail.

The group control differs from the control who works individually, in that, the group works together and the whole force of the group goes to give the result. The individual control is usually a junior member of the group, and does not date back as far as most members of the group, and returns to do special work of a detailed character.

How We on Our Side Contact the Control

Now you may want to know how we, on our side see and feel the control at a sitting. We are conscious of a presence, much larger, more vast than ourselves, which seems to overshadow and encircle the sitting. In other words, all lesser and evil influences are shut out by the great masses of the group that form the control. Great masses of spiritual presences, did I say? Yes, a multitude of the heavenly host, if you like to view them in that light. A Mass that has decided to return and work in the Universe it has left rather than pass over the threshold where its individuality is absorbed in the House of God.

The Linking Up of the Spheres

The controls who come back to Earth are a link between your sphere and the next. Others work the interval between the third and fourth spheres, and so on until the whole Universe, as we know it, is united by these masses of spiritual presences. The linking up of the Earth with the sphere above it is the most difficult of our tasks. To plunge into the Earth atmosphere needs a much greater effort than to plunge into the atmosphere of the third or fourth spheres. That is why your link is a small and fragile one. There is much greater evidence of continued life in the spheres above you. You must take what you get, and be far more thankful for it than you are, in consideration of all the toil that produces it for you.

The controls and guides do more for you than you know. They console you for the loss of your loved ones, and give you the hope and assurance of a future life. They do much more than that, they secure you a safe passage through the spheres. If you have come in contact with them, you will not doubt that eternal life is yours.

Service – a Matter of Free will

You ask: do these groups continue long in the service of the lower spheres? Is a time appointed for them to pass into the unknown? No it is a matter of free will. If they *do not wish* to be merged into the whole, if they are satisfied to continue as members of groups, they can do so. There is no dictatorship in the seventh sphere. When you reach that, you are master of your own destiny. Perhaps you will ask, are these groups angels? Yes they are, and yet, behind them, there may be Archangels greater than themselves. The merging of personality, into the personality of others makes for strength and gives power. In their own sphere, the controls are very powerful, and yet must obey certain laws set for their community.

Definition of the Word "Soul".

Here I must remind you that the word soul, which you use so glibly, designates, not the inner lining of the human being which will survive his death, but a great mass of spirit which is always in the spheres above him, and which has knowledge of the universe which the human being functioning on Earth has not. The souls of all the living, whom you call dead, are always in the higher spheres. Each step they take on their journey, means an extension of consciousness, and yet they know all though they can only use part. So all of you, living men and women, belong to groups, and are, in a sense, potential guides.

Your Responsibility to Your Soul

Consider your responsibility to your own soul. Do you want to keep it in the lower spheres, or do you want it to rise and merge itself into its group? The soul must hunger for the company of its fellows. You may say: "Yes but in many cases the effort is too great." Sloth is the worst sin that can be committed. A slothful soul is worse than a wicked one, because it has not even the activity to sin. It moves neither backwards nor forwards, and has no desire to join its fellows. Eventually the soul must force itself to rise from the Earth, but there are cases when the individual returns again and again to the world. Not in the same body perhaps, but with the same desires and emotions. It comes back because it has no wish to change its condition. It may remain in the world for thousands of years. But eventually, the soul must realize its backward condition. The awakening may come during the Earth incarnation, or in the interval between two lives. It is generally accomplished through the assistance of the guide who sees this waste, and makes a violent effort to force the desires of the sleeping soul. Here you have a new function of the control. The awakening or stimulating of the soul. The control, or guide is anxious to force the undeveloped soul through its seven stages of consciousness, so that it may rejoin the group from which it was taken, they cannot function unless the living human being opens a way for them. In isolated cases they may force their way through, but in the majority, the living soul must co-operate, as in the case of hypnosis.

To conclude my chapter on the controls, I shall speak of them as Masters or Teachers of the Universe. The Universe is governed by them. They work of course, under certain laws, but they have very much more free will as to the length of time they will live, before they lose their individuality, than any inhabitants of the lower spheres.

They frequently call themselves Master or Teacher or Messenger. These are vague terms, but these guides are essential for your development. They are ready to help you in any way, which will help the ends for which they have contacted you. Remember however, that if they give you council or help, it is always with this end in view. Obey them, so far as their advice affects your psychic and spiritual development, but keep your own counsel in practical matters.

Questions and Answers

Q. Do you see Johannes? (Mrs. Dowden's Control.)

A. Not clearly, but I am very conscious of his presence and he can speak to me.

Q. Do you see White Hawk? (Mrs. Barkel's Control.)

A. Yes, as a shape, a form much bigger than myself. As a shape which seems to bend over the sitting and almost enclose it.

Q. Do the individual Controls belong to a group too?

A. Yes. But detach themselves from it, and do their work alone at the sittings. Johannes is a huge group, he works through all the members of his circle.

Q. Is White Hawk a group?

A. Yes, he is a huge Red Indian group. Feda is an individual control working away from her own group.

Q. What about Dodo, the little girl who helps at the sittings of the Misses Moore? She says she only passed over a few years ago.

A. Quite true. She is used as a mouthpiece. She has others working through her, and with her. Used by a group of small controls.

Q. Have the small controls travelled through the seven spheres?

A. No they haven't. They must work through a centre spirit who has had that experience.

Q. Fletcher, Mr. Ford's control, is he a mouthpiece?

A. Yes, used as a method of attracting your attention. His personality is working with a group.

Q. Feda, has she passed through the seven spheres? (Mrs. Leonard's Control.)[13]

A. Yes, she has, and is working on her own, but again she takes the grandmother as her mouthpiece.

Q. Why are there so many Red Indians?

A. For this reason, they being very primitive people, and having had their civilization in a very remote age, form a large group for this work. They are very old, have not been in this world for thousands of years. Many of them choose to come back for the sake of the experience.

Q. You say that evil influences are shut out, but they seem to creep in sometimes.

A. This happens always before, never after, the group has taken hold of its medium: these lesser influences step in while the long file, which constitutes the group is passing in.

Q. Influences round a man, who undoubtedly had power, but whose results degenerated, until he was caught cheating.

---

[13] See *My Life in Two Worlds* by Mrs. Leonard. Stead Library.

A. That is quite a different matter. In a case like that, it is the medium's fault. He is working against his group and they can no longer protect him. The medium must give full consent if the group is to act.

Q. Is there consciousness in the interval between two lives?

A. Yes, but not consciousness in the sense it would be were the soul ready to rise.

The Great Subconscious Mind

Note. – (The following was given through at a sitting with Miss Cummins. I include it here as I feel it is important, and will be helpful to investigators, and to Spiritualists generally. – E.W.S.) W.T.S. With reference to communication I should like to explain one difficulty more clearly. There is here a great subconscious mind. Just as you have a subliminal self whilst in the physical body, we have it here also. We deposit most of our Earth memories for facts in it, so you can realize our difficulty in telling the facts of our life when we communicate, for as your memory for facts lies mostly in your subconscious, so does ours, and this explains the difficulty of giving evidence.

E.W.S. You told us that the facts of your life are very clear, are, as it were, laid out on a table before you.

W.T.S. I have only to enter into my subconscious mind, which is also mingling with others, or rather connected with them, and I can tap the great reservoir of memory, but not easily when I am communicating, then I am in a slightly hypnotized state. It is quite pleasant and sometimes most refreshing, but it is not the same as the ordinary consciousness. One part of me is drowsy, and the other, the deeper part, is very much awake. It is one of the subjective states over here. I have been talking to Myers about it, and he agrees with me. It means that certain facts can be given through by us when communicating. There is another point that is important. We can enter into the subconscious minds of the living, and under such conditions we see what things you have been doing. Actually to claim that we are always with you is not correct. When we enter into the deeper mind of one dear to us, we are very much with that one. It is like an open book. We read the page, and we often say: "I was with you yesterday, and saw you go to such and such a place" or "saw you at your breakfast" – any mundane fact you like, which does seem to testify to our being constantly with you. But as time is different, we are really only with you, as we get the impression of the event, we describe in opening the page, seeing it in your deeper mind. I know this point has been a difficult one with you, you have argued it with someone, somewhere, for I see the argument in your deeper mind. Young spirits actually think they are with their dear ones continually because, when they enter into their subliminal mind, they do not realize that their impression is instantaneous, according to your time, but not according to ours.

You will find in the actual physical mind a map or explanation, of our physical mentality. In the brain are centres which control certain parts of the body, actual groups of cells, that function without your conscious knowledge of their acts. You understand that. Very well, then, apply that to a discarnate mentality. I, for instance, have certain centres that travel to my friends on Earth and to other worlds. Sometimes my ordinary consciousness knows little or nothing about it, just as those in the physical body, know little or nothing of the way the brain centres direct the functions of the body almost mechanically.

My various psychic centres have born messages to many when I did not go to them personally.

White and Black Magic

The fundamental fact of the Universe is sex and procreation, and this subject is closely connected with both black and white magic.

Imagine sex as the root of a great tree whose branches reach up to the clouds. It has provided the tree with its power to grow. The roots are perhaps, not so beautiful as the trunk and branches, but without the root the tree could have no being. If the root is sound it spreads and grows, and the tree shoots up and remains beautiful for many seasons: but if the root is rotten it infects the Earth with decayed matter and foul insects infest it.

If sex is rightly and justly used and, I should add, looked on as a perfectly natural function, which is also the root of spiritual love, then sex may be glorified. Its symbols may be used for the benefit of man and it may be a beatific power. But if it is perverted, if sex and its symbols are used for evil purposes, if the function of creation is turned against the soul of men, it can be a terrible power for evil.

Its symbols can be used – and guides of mediums know how to use them. They can be a gigantic power for good and evil.

Playing with fire describes this feebly.

Questions and Answers

Q. In what particular way do symbols work?

A. Words are symbols which taken in groups, convey thoughts. There are forces, mighty forces, outside your world which can destroy, or stamp obsessing entities. If the guide shows the symbol that can summon any of these forces into activity, the obsessor is no more likely to stay than if you, suddenly finding a patient ill with cholera, beside you, would risk infection by remaining near it.

Q. Is the symbol used as a link, or is it efficacious in itself?

A. It is not efficacious in itself.

Degrees and Kinds of Madness

Q. Can you give some explanation of the different causes of madness?

A. This word madness which is used very glibly, covers a multitude of disorders, which vary quite as much as bodily ailments. There are so many degrees and kinds of madness, that even the most eminent of your alienists, have only classified them in a rough and ready manner. Even the minor forms can be classified under a multitude of different headings. Take the form of mental disorder, common in young women, which is usually attributed to disappointed love, and rightly so, unfortunately those who undertake the treatment are not aware of the true state of affairs. Disappointed love is largely physical; it is still alive and full of vigour. Though it has been thwarted it does not die easily, but it transfers itself. It invariably reshapes into a different symbol of sex. Love, being partly physical, and partly spiritual, has a life in the sphere above its own. If the physical expression is thwarted, it draws itself into its spiritual counterpart, and the soul no longer functions with the body in a normal manner. The symbol it takes, is either the mother or the child, and so intense is the concentration on this, that the girl in her daily life, will believe (and this is not a delusion in the full sense of the word) that either she is a mother, or that she is protected, as an infant is by a spiritual mother. She has transferred this part of herself to the sphere above her, and has actually created the situation in which she believes. The same condition, may take refuge in religion, but there again it has drawn itself up into the spiritual, and if it continues to do so, the spiritual delusion on Earth will merely be the expression of the situation on the sphere above. The commonest form of religious mania, is when the sufferers imagine themselves to be one of the saints, the Virgin Mary or even Jesus Christ. When this occurs, the soul is conscious that it has drawn itself into the spheres above, and the lower portion of it, is conscious of its own expansion.

These cases can be treated by suggestion to the soul itself, when the patient is asleep, and the soul as a whole is normal. It can then understand that the body requires its full due of consciousness.

In other forms of mania, where there is no drawing up of the spirit, such as that the patient is a pail of water, a bottle or any concrete object, it means that the soul and body are not functioning together, that the soul is half detached from the body, and the last thing seen in the normal condition, remains in the memory.

Melancholia is the form of madness that is easiest to cure. What happens when the patient hasn't a single ray of hope left either in Earth or heaven? In that case the soul has been drawn into the astral web of dreams. The cord between body and soul is still unbroken, so that death has not occurred. The body is functioning practically without the soul. But the soul can be freed from the web if the right treatment is employed. In fact, most cases of melancholia could be cured quickly if the patient were hypnotized, then, when the body was passive, in a state of deep trance, the soul could be induced to enter it fully and completely. In such a case the trance would last for many hours, but the patient would, on awakening be cured. On the other hand, if the melancholic condition remains for a long period, and no effort is made to cure it, the brain may change, because it is lying dormant, like a clock that has run down. Then the case is hopeless.

I cannot attempt to particularize the vast mass of mental disorders, but I shall try to point out in a general way, the cause of madness. The criminal is a madman, whose senses have mastered his reasoning powers. Some cases of mania are merely cases of exaggerated criminal tendency, but some are not, for the enemies without are there, who are always watching for an empty house to live in. These are cases of obsession. You may ask how it is possible to distinguish criminal tendency from obsession. When the patient is obsessed, the entire personality changes. This may occur gradually or suddenly. The intruder is without, and may at first be satisfied with mere suggestions to the patient. He may enter the new house by degrees, or he may rush in, and cause a desperate upheaval, such cases are the most violent ones. In no case of criminal tendency can you have the frenzy of obsession. When that happens, when the padded room and the strait-waistcoat are necessary, the patient is invaded.

It is lamentable to think, that people who are unfortunate enough to suffer from invasion, are not treated in the right way, because the doctors refuse to listen to those on our side who can see what has taken place and can suggest a remedy. The intruder will remain in the body of the patient forever, unless he is expelled, and that can only be done by the use of certain symbols which terrify him into flight.

Many patients who are incarcerated in asylums at the present time, might be normal men and women, if we were allowed to use certain forms of exorcism, but those who have the criminal tendency in themselves will not give way to such treatment. It would be futile to attempt their cure in the same way as that used for the obsessed.

Q. Can it be a combination of the two, obsession and criminal tendency?

A. It can, but seldom is. As a rule it is one or the other, the commonest is obsession.

Q. What are obsessing entities?

A. There are three kinds, first, idle spiritual presences who have no fixed occupation. Their obsessions are usually futile and harmless, such as poltergeist hauntings. Secondly, there are the souls who inhabit the web of the astral or lower planes of the sphere above the Earth. These presences are highly dangerous. They are inexperienced. They watch for a chance, when the soul is absent from the body, when they can enter and hold the fortress securely. These are the worst cases: mania and similar conditions are all due to these human forces in captivity. Thirdly, there are obsessing entities who are not human, and who fill the soul with dreams and fancies. Fixed ideas come under this category.

Q. What type of entities would these be?

A. They are nature spirits who desire to have the experience of inhabiting a body, and who unbalance the mind and give the sufferer fixed ideas. Now if you consider what I have said you will see that the soul is liable to three different kinds of invasion. This is a rough classification. I might truthfully say that there are twenty different forms of invasion, for the nature of these entities differ so much: but I speak of the three broad headings under which you will find them.

You will never find that any entity, human or otherwise, can invade a body unless the soul has, in a sense, given its consent. This seems a strange statement, but it is true. No one suffers from madness who has not allowed his soul to slip away from him for long periods. Those who do not think, suffer from madness: the empty mind is a dangerous thing.

Q. Sometimes it is said that the brain was too clever and caused madness: genius being akin to madness.

A. Yes that is true. In a sense genius lends itself to madness because it has allowed the soul to stray at unsuitable times into the higher sphere. People who can be described as clever (not ultra-clever like geniuses) are seldom mad.

Q. Why are obsessing entities allowed to interfere at sittings?

A. The obsessing entity invariably enters the swollen head. If the head is normal the entity gets no entrance.

Q. How does the soul hang away from the body?

A. The soul withdraws itself from the body and remains outside it. The cord is stretched – a different condition from that of sleep. Then the soul stands close by waiting a chance to come back.

Q. Doesn't Dr. Wickland[14] remove the obsessing entities without the use of symbols or exorcism?

---

[14] See *Thirty Years Amongst the Dead*, by Carl A. Wickland

A. In his case the guides do the exorcism. He merely makes it easier for the invader to get out. The passing through the wife's body is merely a method of making the departure more definite, showing that the invader is expelled twice.

The Power of Mind to Converse with Mind While Still in the Body

The human mind while still functioning through the physical brain possesses a power which has not been generally recognized. It is not known that mind can converse with mind, while still in the body. This is a fact which will be appreciated later on. The word telepathy, or thought transference, does not express my meaning. I mean that minds can converse with each other. It is not a case of transmitter and receiver. When this fact is fully understood, it will become part of the child's education, to be trained mentally to communicate with others.

The process takes place in the following manner: A, wishes to talk to B. A sits down passively, and allows his inner body to escape. The soul body of A then converses with B. This is a conversation between two living persons, and although you can call it telepathy, if you like that word, it has a different meaning to thought transference.

The living can be trained to converse in this way, and when it comes into general practice, it will do away with telephonic communication. Science will discover it, and invent courses of training and mental suggestion that will cultivate this power in the child from its early stages onwards. It will be evolved slowly as the child grows older, it would almost be impossible to use it at the present time.

Q. Could it be done now?

A. Yes, but it would be a great effort for the adult to acquire it, but if the child were trained in its infancy, it would be quite natural.

FINIS

212

www.ingramcontent.com/pod-product-compliance
Lightning Source LLC
Chambersburg PA
CBHW030824090426
42737CB00009B/859